# Sausage

# Sausage

## Recipes for Making and Cooking with Homemade Sausage

VICTORIA WISE

PHOTOGRAPHY BY
LEO GONG

TEN SPEED PRESS
Berkeley

Copyright © 2010 by Victoria Wise
Photographs copyright © 2010 by Leo Gong

All rights reserved.
Published in the United States by Ten Speed Press, an
imprint of the Crown Publishing Group, a division of
Random House, Inc., New York.
www.crownpublishing.com
www.tenspeed.com

Ten Speed Press and the Ten Speed Press colophon are
registered trademarks of Random House, Inc.

Library of Congress Cataloging-in-Publication Data on file
with publisher.

ISBN 978-1-58008-012-5

Printed in China

Design by Katy Brown
Food styling by Karen Shinto

10 9 8 7 6 5 4 3 2 1

First Edition

FOR MY HUSBAND, RICK WISE,
*life mate, helpmate, and dining companion for more than three decades who, thank heaven, never tires of sausage.*

# CONTENTS

# ACKNOWLEDGMENTS

I ADORE Ten Speed Press, their style, their expertise, their attitude, the gorgeous books they publish, and, of course, their perspicacity in choosing to publish this one. It was especially gratifying to work with Aaron Wehner, publisher, who spotted this project's worth, and with Melissa Moore, project editor for this book, and Dawn Yanagihara, end-stage editor, both of whom are unflappably cool and collected and on top of the moment no matter the author's concern. Also, Sharon Silva, copy editor par excellence, whose keen reading saved me more than once from potential embarrassment, and Kathy Hashimoto, one of the calmest contract-department persons I have ever encountered. And, for such a beautiful book, thanks many times over to Leo Gong, Karen Shinto, Nancy Austin, and Katy Brown.

In addition, I owe thanks forever to those who bolster and encourage me and without whom I couldn't live in either my professional or personal life. Martha Casselman, my dear friend and former agent before she retired, who encouraged me to get into this crazy business of writing cookbooks and who is still at the ready to help smooth my prose in draft after draft. Susanna Hoffman, dear friend for forty years and sometimes coauthor, with whom I have shared many sausage discussions as we developed cookbooks together and learned from each other. Arayah Jenanyan, my beloved sister, who has a palate uncompromised by personal preference and who, from the beginning until the day we closed the Pig, was key in making sure the meats and vegetables in the display case shined clear and fresh, as well as in keeping me and the rest of the shop focused throughout the day. James "Chooch" Potenziani, the master behind the art and finesse of turning out the divine sausages, pâtés, hams, and other charcuterie that made the Pig renowned before the word *charcuterie* became hip in the American food lexicon. Penny Brogden, artist and friend, who energetically lent her artistic sensibility and hands-on effort to the daily operations of making beautiful and delicious food at the Pig. This sausage cookbook has grown from all of them.

# INTRODUCTION

I HAVE ALWAYS BEEN FASCINATED by sausage: how the simple notion of finely chopped and salted meat, primarily pork, has changed over time to include poultry, seafood, and vegetarian variations. But no wonder it has evolved. Sausage does double duty, providing affordable everyday sustenance for the family table and doable, interesting fare for sophisticated entertaining.

In 1973, I opened Pig-by-the-Tail, a French-style delicatessen, in what was to become Berkeley's famed Gourmet Ghetto. My intent and dream was to bring charcuterie back to the American marketplace, from which it had long been missing. In the latter part of the nineteenth century, a huge variety of sausages were available at local butcher shops. But by the 1970s, little was offered in the way of locally made fresh sausages. Neighborhood butcher shops and delicatessens that had routinely sold their own house-cured hams and fresh sausages had seen their

role taken over by commercial enterprises proffering so-called fresh sausages, either laced with the additives necessary to keep them safe to eat or "previously frozen" to keep them "fresh" in transport from factory to supermarket. Such products continue to service a broad range of clients, but they do so at the cost of flavor and succulence.

Yet, the taste for straight-from-the-neighborhood sausages remained. The fresh sausages sold at Pig-by-the-Tail, which were French-style at the outset, in keeping with the charcuterie theme, were an instant hit.

Our selection quickly expanded to include Italian, Spanish, German, middle European, and Russian variations. We turned eastward to the beloved dishes of *kufta* I know from my Armenian heritage, where lamb and bulgur meatballs done dozens of ways were customarily made for family occasions. More sausages were discovered as we moved farther east and south to Syria and Lebanon and then north to the Caucasus. And as long as we were on the road, why not continue to Southeast Asia and China? Or, why not head directly north from central Europe and sample British and Scandinavian ways with sausage? Including all of those sausage permutations in the repertoire was a natural. And our customers loved them.

As early as Roman times, the classical cookery text of Apicius pointed out the myriad possibilities of sausage expressions, from meat to fish to fowl to a sweet fruit-filled version. It is not surprising that Apicius has become a darling of modern food writers and chefs, me among them, who delight in his somewhat freewheeling prose that describes without prescribing or proscribing, leaving plenty of room for innovation.

Following Apicius's lead as I scouted the world for sausage dishes and delved into their history, I have enlarged my originally limited notion of casings as animal intestines to include wraps and containers of many kinds: scaloppine rolls, vegetable containers (tomatoes, eggplants, bell peppers, zucchini), leafy wraps (cabbage, grape, fig, and lettuce leaves), ready-made Chinese wonton squares for ravioli, and Southeast Asian rice paper rounds for spring rolls. I have also come to embrace the notion of sausages with no casing at all. Balls, patties, and fritters, with or without meat, are now all part of my world of sausages.

Sausages present the cook with an ever-changing landscape of possibilities. Rustic to ritzy, homey to haute, they can be eaten any time of the day: breakfast, lunch, afternoon snack, dinner, midnight nibble. Pound for pound, and used either as background or as the star of a dish, they are economical, too: a small amount of meat with other provender can stretch to provide a bountiful meal.

I have tailored the recipes in this book so that no special grinding and stuffing equipment is required to turn out delicious, good-looking sausages. On the other hand, if you want to honor tradition and stuff your sausage into an animal casing—and I often still do for some preparations—the appendix (page 153) provides all you will need to know.

Each sausage recipe includes one or more ways to use what you've made, sometimes with one or more simple accompaniments, but most often within a dish. All in all, the recipes are part of a repertoire that began at Pig-by-the-Tail and continues to live on in this book. It is a celebration of sausages and my outside-the-box approach to making them. Enjoy.

# INGREDIENTS

YOU DON'T HAVE TO STOCK UP on exotic ingredients to use the recipes in this book. On the contrary, nearly all the ingredients are familiar and readily available. Here's what you'll need for making the sausages and for cooking the dishes that include them. The first part covers store-bought ingredients, and the second describes homemade ones.

## Store-Bought Ingredients

### Meats

Use meats, preferably organic, with a moderate amount of fat. If purchasing ground meat, it should have at least 15 percent fat and no more than 20 percent. If it has more, the texture of the sausage will be too soft. How finely or coarsely the meat is ground is also important. In general, a medium grind is what you want. Lamb routinely comes in a medium grind. Beef does, too, except for so-called chili grind, which is too large to soften into a tender sausage. Ground pork is generally more problematic. It is often excessively trimmed of fat to suit the no-fat mindset that currently prevails, and is too finely ground for making sausages with sufficient texture. Amending pork that is too finely ground with minced fat solves the problem, which is how the recipes in this book return succulence and texture to finely ground lean pork. Or, of course, you can grind your own meat. See page 153 for information on which cuts to use.

1

## Fats

**Pork Back Fat** Pork back fat, also called fatback, barding fat, and in German *speck*, is the fat that runs along a pig's back. It is the preferred fat for sausages, both for its flavor and because it sets up well after cooking, providing succulence without flabbiness. It is not readily available in markets. But, if you purchase pork loin or pork butt untrimmed, you can trim them and stockpile the fat in the freezer to use in place of back fat for making sausages. However, that is a considerable chore for slow gain.

**Leaf Lard** Leaf lard, the delicious, hard fat from around the kidneys, is also suitable for sausages, though it, too, is hard to come by. It can sometimes be special ordered, or you might check with pork purveyors at farmers' markets, who are typically devoted to pasture raising, humanely slaughtering, and using the whole hog.

**Salt Pork** To substitute for back fat or leaf lard, I use salt pork, the fat from the belly with striations of meat running through it. It is not as hard as back fat, but it is almost as satisfactory for sausages. Lean pork belly is used for bacon, the meat bands being what is wanted. For sausages, it is the opposite: the fat is the prize, so choose pieces that have the most fat. There are several brands of salt pork on the market, usually sold in vacuum-wrapped blocks of about 6 ounces. Some come still crusted in salt; some come basically desalted. The former needs to be rinsed several times and then blanched in boiling water for 5 minutes to leech out the salt. The latter is ready to go, with the proviso that you must be judicious when adding salt to the recipe. That's an easy call: cook a small sample of the sausage mixture, taste it, and continue from there. In recipes that call for salt pork, I have included a line that reminds you to test for saltiness before you add more salt.

The most facile way to mince salt pork without a meat grinder is to freeze it partially, enough so that a knife blade glides through it without mashing it. Then use a chef's knife or food processor, first cutting it into small pieces, to chop it as finely as possible.

**Oils** I almost always use extra virgin olive oil. Some years ago, this seemed rather fancy and imprudent for everyday use. That was then. Nowadays, many, many extra virgin olive oils are available. They range from not so expensive to quite pricy. For cooking, I use a medium-priced extra virgin oil. Lesser grades are not worth the money you pay for the word *olive* on the label. Instead, when I want a vegetable oil other than olive oil, I use peanut oil. It has more viscosity, which means it is not as thin and watery as many other vegetable oils, such as canola or corn oil, and it has a high smoke point, making it a good choice for high-heat sautéing or frying. Many brands of peanut oil are on the market, and they vary in how much flavor they impart to a dish. I use a neutrally flavored peanut oil, rather than a more full-flavored, expeller-expressed artisanal product. A note of caution: keep in mind that peanut oil is potentially very harmful for those who are allergic to peanuts. When in doubt, use canola oil.

**Butter** Heretical though it may sound, the difference between salted and unsalted butter is not of as much importance to me as it is to, say, a pastry chef. In general, for savory dishes, the nuance of salt in salted butter does not interfere with other tastes. I have tried many high-end, expensive domestic and imported butters and found that most are not worth the price. There is an exception. I love Parmigiano-Reggiano butter, which comes from the region where Parmigiano-Reggiano cheese is produced. It is made from cream collected from the same dairy cows that produce milk for the manufacture of the world-famous cheese. Other than butter that you might make yourself, this is the one that best retains the sweetness of truly fresh farmstead butter. Unfortunately, it is dear, maybe even a little exorbitant, so I reserve it for uses where the butter is key, as in butter sauces or for slathering on bread. For everyday cooking, I choose a good-quality domestic organic butter, either salted or unsalted.

## Herbs
For the most part, I purchase herbs fresh. But experience has taught me that fresh herbs do not keep well. Indeed, no matter how they are refrigerated—wrapped in paper towels or stood in a glass of water—they will begin to rot after 4 or 5 days. So, as soon as a fresh herb bundle shows signs of deteriorating, I untie it, place it in a small bowl, and set it in the cupboard, uncovered, so it can slowly air dry. Then, I use it at whatever stage it is at the moment I need a teaspoon or so for the dish I am cooking. I have found this to be a very satisfactory way to have fresh herbs and freshly dried herbs always on hand. Keep in mind that dried herbs are more concentrated in flavor, so if a recipe calls for 1 teaspoon of a fresh herb and what you have is dry or almost dry, use only $\frac{1}{2}$ teaspoon.

## Spices
Volumes have been devoted to spices and their magical, commercial, curative, and culinary powers. Here, in brief, I will say only that I keep a shelf filled with spices, arranged in alphabetical order so they're easy to pull out for a recipe without fumbling through the whole cupboard. I buy them in small amounts and keep them in tightly capped jars so they stay fresh for several months.

## Salt and Pepper
For cooking, I use kosher salt because it is inexpensive and flows freely without the use of additives. Fine sea salt is also a good choice, but if you opt for it, pull back on the measurement a bit: 1 teaspoon kosher salt is equal to $\frac{3}{4}$ teaspoon fine sea salt. For condiment salt, I enjoy the sizes, shapes, and colors of salt crystals, which can be found in gourmet

markets. They are expensive, however, and other than the fun you can have discerning minimal taste differences, I don't find one type is a better choice than another. So, I have settled on *sel gris* from the Brittany coast of France, where the salt beds have been tended as lovingly as a garden for centuries. Its gray (*gris*) color comes from the clay in the shallow marshes where it is harvested. It is moist and has medium-size soft crystals, so that it melts in the mouth and then disappears before intruding its presence on the dish it is garnishing. Unlike other condiment salts, *sel gris* is also a fine cooking salt because it readily and smoothly blends into its surround, leaving no trace of its crystalline origin. Also, it is not expensive so you can use it expansively.

I employ mostly black peppercorns but use white peppercorns when I don't want black specks to be visible in the mix. There is not a huge taste difference between black and white pepper, except that white is a little more nutty and softer on the tongue than black pepper. I also sometimes use green peppercorns, which are elusively herby and at the same time peppery. I always grind peppercorns to order.

# Homemade Ingredients

## Fresh Bread Crumbs

There's no reason to settle for the sorry excuse for bread crumbs available commercially. All you need to make your own is a food processor and some day-old bread.

Since I use *a lot* of bread crumbs in my cooking, I use my freezer for stockpiling bits and pieces from unfinished loaves, eventually to be turned into crumbs. In fact, if I'm out of my freezer inventory, I deliberately "stale" fresh bread for crumb making by drying it out in a low oven until it's no longer squeezable. The best bread for all-purpose crumbs is *bâtard*, *ciabatta*, or a similar artisanal French or Italian bread without seeds, walnuts, olives, or the like.

To make bread crumbs, cut off most of the crust, leaving a little on for texture, then cut the bread into roughly 1-inch chunks. Place the chunks in the food processor bowl up to the top of the blade knob—no higher or the bread will turn into a glob rather than crumbs. Use pulses to swirl the chunks until the crumbs are as fine as you like. If you want extra-fine crumbs, such as what you might use for coating food on which you want a particularly crisp crust, briefly dry the chunks in a low oven (325°F) until firm but not toasted, then cool and process. Store any crumbs you won't be using within 2 or 3 days in the freezer.

## Broths

As much as I dote on long-cooked, lovingly tended meat stocks in the Continental style of the last two centuries, in the less preponderated fare of today, I opt for lighter broths, specifically chicken broth and vegetable broth. They must be homemade. Canned won't do. Here are my easy ways to make them.

## CHICKEN BROTH

**MAKES 12 TO 14 CUPS (3 TO 3½ QUARTS)**

Homemade broth makes a world of difference for the better in any dish that calls for chicken broth. Happily, a light and flavorful one can be made with only chicken backs and wings and water, no other elements—carrots, onions, celery, herbs—required, and briefly simmered for one unattended hour. It's worth making a large amount to have on hand because it stores well in the refrigerator under the protective layer of fat that solidifies on the surface when it is chilled. If the fat seal is not broken, the broth will keep for 3 weeks in the refrigerator. If you break the fat to use just part of the broth, reheat the remainder until the fat melts completely, then cool and refrigerate it, checking to be sure the fat seals the entire surface again. The broth can also be frozen for up to 6 months. In this case, the fat layer prevents ice crystals from forming across the surface. For thrift, I use backs and wings for broth.

But, you can also employ legs, thighs, and breasts, use them to make the broth, then remove them to serve as part of another dish.

> 5 pounds chicken backs and wings
> or other parts

Place the chicken parts in a pot large enough to hold them submerged as they cook. Add water to cover by 2 inches and bring just to a boil over medium heat. Adjust the heat to maintain a gentle simmer (don't let it boil at full speed or you will have murky broth), partially cover the pot, and cook for 1 hour.

Strain through a fine-mesh sieve and cool completely. Or, cool completely in the pot, then strain into storage containers. Refrigerate uncovered until chilled. Without removing the fat, cover and store in the refrigerator for up to 3 weeks (if the fat seal is not broken) or in the freezer for up to 6 months. Just before using, lift off the layer of solidified fat from the surface.

## VEGETABLE BROTH

**MAKES ABOUT 10 CUPS (2½ QUARTS)**

Contrary to what you might think, making a fine vegetable broth is not a matter of tossing any vegetable matter into a pot and boiling it up. The vegetables you start with need not be picture perfect, but starchy vegetables, such as potatoes, should not be part of the mix or the broth will turn out murky, and brassicas, like cabbage and broccoli, are also not good to use or the broth will not be clear tasting. Then, don't stint on the amount of vegetables for the amount of broth you would like to wind up with. One tomato and one chard leaf do not a tasty broth make. There should be enough water so that the vegetables barely float, but not any more. Cook the broth until the vegetables are very soft but not disintegrating; this helps make a clear broth. Following is a mix and method I use to make a good-size batch of vegetable broth that is rich enough to serve on its own as a bouillon or use as a base for any soup.

4 tomatoes, coarsely cut up

1 small yellow or white onion, coarsely cut up

2 large cloves garlic

1 rib celery, coarsely cut up

1 carrot, coarsely cut up

1 zucchini, coarsely cut up

2 cups coarsely shredded leafy greens, such as chard, spinach, dandelion, or hearty lettuce, or a mixture

8 to 10 fresh parsley sprigs

6 fresh cilantro sprigs

2 fresh thyme sprigs or ½ teaspoon dried thyme

1 small bay leaf

1 teaspoon kosher salt

10 cups (2½ quarts) water

In a large pot, combine all the ingredients, cover partially, and bring to a boil over high heat. Decrease the heat to maintain a brisk simmer and cook until the vegetables are very soft and the broth is well colored, about 1 hour.

Strain through a fine-mesh sieve and cool completely. Or, cool completely in the pot, then strain into storage containers. Refrigerate uncovered until chilled. Cover and store in the refrigerator for up to 3 days or in the freezer for up to 3 weeks.

# BASIC STEAMED RICE

**MAKES ABOUT 2 CUPS**

Rice, plainly steamed, is an underpinning, accompaniment, or ingredient for many dishes, both in this book and in kitchens around the world. In order to avoid the confusion that can result because of the many kinds of rice available, I have come to rely on a basic method for preparing steamed rice that works whether you need cooked rice for adding to a recipe or serving as a side dish. It is easy to do, though you must pay attention to when it comes to a boil and then promptly turn down the heat before it boils over, makes a mess on the stove, and turns out mushy rather than in beautifully individual grains. For other rice recipes in the book, see South African Sausage with Collard Greens, Ethiopian Spiced Butter, and Cashew Rice (page 69), Paella with Chorizo, Shrimp, and Baby Artichokes (page 130), and Brown Rice, Walnut, and Dandelion Green Veg "Sausage" Wrapped in Cabbage Leaves with Tomato-Caper Sauce (page 151).

1 cup long-grain, medium-grain, or short-grain white rice (not converted)
2 cups water

Rinse the rice briefly in a sieve under cold running water, put it in a small, heavy saucepan, add the water, and bring to a boil over medium-high heat. Decrease the heat until the water is barely shuddering. Cover the pot, set the timer for 22 minutes, and let the rice cook without lifting the lid. When the timer sounds, the water will have been absorbed and the rice will be tender.

Remove from the heat and set aside, still covered, to finish cooking and steam dry for 10 minutes, or even longer is okay. Fluff up the rice with a fork just before using or serving.

# Pork Sausages

PORK IS BY FAR the most widely used meat for sausages and their first cousins, meatballs. Wherever pigs can be raised and are not proscribed by religious law, pig meat, head to tail, inside and out, prevails. It is an animal that provides a reverential amount of food for the table, both in its largesse and in its taste. Pork also opens its arms wide to a world of culinary interpretations. French, Italian, Spanish, Chinese, and Southeast Asian cooks have exploited its possibilities for centuries and elevated its culinary renderings to one of the high arts of cooking. Elsewhere, in South America, Africa, and Russia, cooks also revere the pig, although with a scarcer supply. So, I begin this sausage journey with pig tales and pig recipes.

# American Breakfast Sausage

Breakfast sausage, in patties or links, is a staple of the great American breakfast plate. It's an important player in the hearty, stoke-up-for-the-day meal that includes eggs, cooked anyway you'd like; toast or pancakes; and mugs of hot java. It is served on the road as early as 4 a.m. to truckers and workers off to the fields or factories. A bit later, it feeds tourists fueling up for a day's adventure of skiing, mountain climbing, and other energetic activities. And on Sunday mornings, home-style cafes are filled with customers looking to splurge calories on a big breakfast out. But you don't need to stop at breakfast when using this sausage. It also makes a delicious taco filling or pizza topping. As often as not, breakfast sausage is served in patties, but if you prefer links, you can stuff it into sheep casing. **MAKES 1 POUND**

14 ounces ground pork

2 ounces salt pork, fat only, minced

¾ teaspoon rubbed sage (not ground sage)

½ teaspoon dried thyme

½ teaspoon dried marjoram

Scant ¼ teaspoon powdered ginger

¼ teaspoon freshly ground black pepper

⅛ teaspoon cayenne pepper

1 teaspoon kosher salt, or to taste, if needed

Place all the ingredients except the salt in a medium bowl, and knead with your hands until thoroughly blended. Cook and taste a small sample, then add the salt if needed. Leave in bulk and shape as directed in individual recipes or stuff into sheep casing. The sausage can be used right away. (The uncooked sausage will keep in the refrigerator for up to 3 days or in the freezer for up to 1 week.)

Sauté or grill, or cook as directed in individual recipes.

# Rustic Cornmeal Pancakes Dappled with American Breakfast Sausage and Slicked with Maple Syrup

The advantage of including the sausage in the pancake batter is that you don't have to use a second pan to cook the sausage for a side. It saves thermal unit energy, making it eco-friendly, and it saves the energy of the cook because there are fewer dishes to wash. The addition of polenta, which is more coarsely ground than cornmeal, makes for a slightly nubby texture and pleasing "bite." For an everyday breakfast, I usually make the pancakes plate size, but they make a fine stack of dollar-size pancakes, too, if you'd like to go for "more" rather than "bigger." Use about 2 tablespoons for each dollar-size cake; you should end up with about 18 pancakes. The batter, without the added sausage, can be stored in the refrigerator for up to 4 days; just before cooking, stir in the crumbled sausage. Using grade B maple syrup accents the rustic theme. It is also the grade recommended by savvy Vermonters, who prefer its deeper, browner lushness over grade A. **MAKES 6 PLATE-SIZE PANCAKES**

1½ cups yellow cornmeal

½ cup polenta

1½ cups boiling water

¾ cup all-purpose flour

2 teaspoons baking powder

1 tablespoon sugar

¾ teaspoon kosher salt

1 cup milk

1 large egg

3 tablespoons butter, melted

6 ounces American Breakfast Sausage (page 10)

Butter or ghee (see page 71), for cooking the pancakes

Maple syrup, preferably grade B, for serving

To make the pancake batter, place the cornmeal and polenta in a large bowl and slowly pour in the boiling water, whisking to mix it in as you go. Set aside to soften the grains while preparing the remaining ingredients.

In a small bowl, combine the flour, baking powder, sugar, and salt and stir together with a fork. Combine the milk and egg in another small bowl and whisk to mix.

Add the milk mixture and melted butter to the cornmeal mixture and whisk to mix. Whisk in the flour mixture to make a thick, coarse batter. Crumble the sausage and stir it into the batter.

*continued*

Preheat the oven to 250°F. Generously grease a heavy, 8- to 9-inch skillet with the butter and warm it over medium-high heat. Ladle about 1/2 cup of the batter into the skillet and cook until golden on the bottom, about 5 minutes. Flip the cake with a spatula and continue cooking until golden on the second side, 2 to 3 minutes more. Transfer to a baking sheet and place in the oven to keep warm. Continue until all the batter is used.

Place a pancake or two on individual plates and drizzle maple syrup across the top. Serve.

# Pork and Chestnut Sausage

Chestnuts are a cold-weather crop, available from early fall to the end of winter. At that time of year, when the plane trees in Italy's town squares occasionally still have some leaves left from summer and no sign of spring is in sight, vendors set up sidewalk braziers in the piazzas and roast chestnuts over open fires. They are served up right off the grill, piping hot, in newspaper cones. You have to be out and about to get them that way, and bundled in suitably warm clothing to guard against the weather. Once you buy them, it's a slow, peel-as-you-go proposition. But somehow the divine combination of freshly roasted chestnuts and a hot coffee from a nearby stand chases away the cold and lessens the effort necessary to pry off the invariably recalcitrant charred shells and inner skins.

With the already peeled, freeze-dried or vacuum-wrapped chestnuts now available, the pleasure, albeit without the char but also without the chore, is brought to the home kitchen year-round. If you do not use all the chestnuts in the package, freeze the remainder. If you store them in the refrigerator, they will mold after just a few days. **MAKES ¾ POUND**

2 tablespoons butter

½ cup coarsely chopped freeze-dried or vacuum-packed peeled chestnuts

½ cup finely chopped yellow or white onion

1½ tablespoons finely chopped celery

½ teaspoon fresh thyme leaves or ¼ teaspoon dried thyme

Small pinch of freshly grated nutmeg

¼ teaspoon sugar

¼ teaspoon kosher salt

¼ teaspoon freshly ground black pepper

½ pound ground pork

In a large sauté pan, melt the butter over medium heat. Add the chestnuts, onion, celery, thyme, nutmeg, sugar, salt, and pepper and stir to mix. Cook until the vegetables begin to sweat, about 2 minutes. Transfer to a medium bowl and set aside to cool completely.

Add the pork to the cooled chestnut mixture, and knead with your hands until thoroughly blended. Leave in bulk and shape as directed in individual recipes or stuff into hog casing. The sausage can be used right away.

Sauté or grill, or cook as directed in individual recipes. (The uncooked sausage will keep in the refrigerator for up to 3 days; it does not freeze well.)

# Pork and Chestnut Sausage Wrapped in Chicken Breast Scaloppine

Pigs in a blanket was a dish my mother made when it was time for a-something-special for dinner. Customarily, the pigs are sausages and the blankets are biscuit pastry of some sort, sometimes with a band of bacon between the two. My mother favored swathing the sausages in bacon only and cooking the bundles in the oven per the usual method. I was always intrigued to watch the care she took to turn them frequently, making sure they browned and cooked evenly all around. Later in life, I created a more sophisticated rendition: the blankets became chicken scaloppine, the pigs transmogrified to a homemade sausage, and red wine entered the ingredient list—still plenty easy, still plenty special. Pork and chestnut sausage makes the dish quite elegant, but a humbler sausage, such as Toulouse, sweet Italian, or American breakfast sausage is also suitable. The rolls can also be cooled, then sliced and used as part of a charcuterie appetizer plate. **SERVES 6 TO 8**

6 small boneless chicken breast halves with skin

1½ pounds Pork and Chestnut Sausage (page 14)

4 tablespoons butter

¼ teaspoon freshly ground black pepper

3 cups red wine

8 cloves garlic, coarsely chopped

2 teaspoons chopped fresh tarragon or ½ teaspoon dried tarragon

One at a time, place each chicken breast between 2 sheets of waxed paper or plastic wrap. With a mallet or other pounding device, such as the flat side of a hammer or the bottom of a wine bottle, pound the chicken breast until ¼ inch thick or slightly thinner.

Discard the waxed paper. Spread about one-sixth of the sausage lengthwise along the center of each scaloppine. Roll up to enclose the sausage and secure closed with toothpicks or kitchen string.

In a sauté pan large enough to hold the chicken rolls without crowding, melt the butter over medium heat. Add the rolls, sprinkle them with the black pepper, and sauté, turning frequently, until lightly golden all around, 10 to 12 minutes.

Add the wine, garlic, and tarragon and stir to mix. Bring just to a boil and decrease the heat to maintain a gentle simmer. Cook uncovered, basting frequently, until the juices are no longer pink when a roll is pierced, about 15 minutes. Transfer the rolls to a platter and set aside in a warm place.

Reduce the liquid remaining in the pan over high heat until bubbles break from the bottom rather than only across the surface, 3 to 5 minutes. Pour the sauce over the rolls and serve right away.

# Butternut Squash Stuffed with Pork and Chestnut Sausage

Of all the winter squashes, butternut is my favorite. Not only is it easy to peel for soups or gratins, but its flesh is also exceptionally creamy and sweetly invites a sausage filling. Stuffed with pork and chestnut sausage, these squash boats can stand alone as a main course, with steamed rice and a sturdy-leaf green salad for side dishes. They also make a notable side dish for a holiday turkey or crown roast.

For precooking the squash, I like to take the microwave advantage. It's ever so much faster. But for finishing the dish, I use the oven because it produces a toastier, more visually appealing look. **SERVES 4 TO 6**

2 small butternut squashes
  (about 1 pound each)
¾ pound Pork and Chestnut Sausage
  (page 14)

1½ cups fresh bread crumbs (page 4)
2 tablespoons butter, cut into small pieces

Preheat the oven to 400°F.

Cut the squashes in half lengthwise. Place them cut side down on a baking sheet or in a microwave-safe dish. Sprinkle lightly with water, cover loosely, and cook until squeezable but not mushy, about 40 minutes in the oven, or 10 minutes in the microwave. Remove and set aside to cool. Leave the oven on if you have used it, or preheat it now to 400°F if you haven't.

When the squash halves are cool, scoop out and discard the seeds from each half, then make a slit in the flesh along the middle, from the blossom to the stem end of each half, taking care not to cut through the skin. Pry open the slit and push the pulp to the edges. Fill the cavity with sausage, dividing it evenly among the halves and heaping it high. Add a generous helping of bread crumbs on top and dot with butter.

Return the squash halves, filled sides up, to the baking sheet, and pour a little water in the bottom to keep them from drying out. Bake until the sausage is no longer pink in the middle but still moist and the bread crumbs are golden, about 20 minutes. Serve hot.

# Sage and Bourbon Whiskey Sausage with Cherry Tomato Chutney

Bourbon whiskey, a uniquely American spirit, can be used in cooking the same way wine often is in French recipes, as a splash that lends a subtle, aromatic presence and a bit of moisture. A whiskey sausage, with its breath of musty sage, makes a perfect grilling patty for sandwiching in a bun smeared with tomato chutney. Or, you can roll the sausage into small balls and serve them with the chutney as a dipping sauce. Two things distinguish this speedy chutney from bona fide tomato ketchup: its consistency is a little looser and less dense, and it is made in little more than half an hour. It will keep in the refrigerator for up to 2 months before its savor diminishes. Use it also to accompany pork chops or grilled chicken or game. **SERVES 4**

**Sausage**

14 ounces ground pork

2 ounces salt pork, fat only, minced

½ teaspoon finely chopped fresh sage

1 tablespoon tomato paste

2 tablespoons bourbon whiskey

½ teaspoon dry mustard

½ teaspoon freshly ground black, white, or green pepper

½ teaspoon kosher salt, or to taste, if needed

**Chutney**

3 tablespoons extra virgin olive oil

2 tablespoons yellow mustard seeds

⅔ cup finely chopped yellow or white onion

4 cloves garlic, minced or pressed

2 teaspoons chopped jalapeño chile

2 tablespoons peeled and minced fresh ginger

½ teaspoon celery seeds

⅛ teaspoon ground cloves

3½ cups red cherry tomatoes, such as Sweet 100s, or grape tomatoes

1⅓ cups cider vinegar

½ cup packed dark brown sugar

2 teaspoons kosher salt

Buns, split, if making sandwiches

To make the sausage, place all the ingredients except the salt in a medium bowl, and knead with your hands until thoroughly blended. Cook and taste a small sample, then add the salt if needed. Leave in bulk or stuff into hog casing. Cover and refrigerate for at least 1 hour to firm and to blend the flavors, though 4 hours or even overnight is better.

*continued*

To make the chutney, heat the oil in a medium saucepan over medium-high heat. Add the mustard seeds and stir until the seeds begin to pop, about 1 minute. Add all the remaining ingredients, stir to mix, and bring to a boil. Decrease the heat to maintain a brisk simmer and cook, uncovered, until almost all of the liquid is gone but the mixture is still a bit moist, about 35 minutes. Remove from the heat, let cool, cover, and chill slightly before using to allow the flavors to coalesce.

To cook the sausage, prepare a medium-hot grill. If using in bulk, form the sausage into patties each about $1/2$ inch thick and 3 inches in diameter or into balls each about $1^1/4$ inches in diameter.

Place the patties, balls, or links on the grill rack directly over the heat source. Cook, turning once or twice, until no longer pink in the center but still quite moist, 15 minutes or so, depending on the shape and thickness.

If serving the sausage in buns, toast the buns, cut sides down, on the grill for 1 to 2 minutes. Spread each half with some of the chutney and sandwich a sausage patty or link between them. Or, arrange the sausage balls on a warmed platter and serve with the chutney on the side.

# Creole Sausage

In the early eighteenth century, Spanish colonists brought a paprika-and-cayenne-seasoned sausage to Louisiana, where they added fresh red chiles and a dash of vinegar to create what is now known as Creole sausage. It is an assertive sausage that rings out "Let the good times roll!" It dances sprightly in gumbo with shrimp and oysters (page 21) and lends vivacity to a New Orleans plate with crab cakes and Cajun rémoulade (page 128). It is also delicious formed into appetizer-size balls, sautéed, and served with rémoulade for dipping. **MAKES ABOUT 1 POUND**

1 pound ground pork

¼ cup minced yellow or white onion

2 small cloves garlic, minced or pressed

¾ teaspoon minced fresh small red or green chile

2 teaspoons cider or red wine vinegar

1 teaspoon hot or sweet Hungarian paprika

½ teaspoon dried thyme

½ small bay leaf, vein removed, leaf finely chopped

1½ teaspoons kosher salt

¼ teaspoon freshly ground black pepper

⅛ teaspoon cayenne pepper

Place all the ingredients in a medium bowl, and knead with your hands until thoroughly blended. Use in bulk and shape as directed in individual recipes or stuff into sheep casing. Cover and refrigerate for at least 3 hours, or preferably overnight to firm and blend the flavors.

Sauté or grill, or cook as directed in individual recipes. (The uncooked sausage will keep in the refrigerator for up to 5 days, or in the freezer for up to 3 weeks.)

# Creole Sausage, Shrimp, and Oyster Gumbo

Sausage in a gumbo usually means smoked sausage. Sometimes Louisiana smoked ham, called tasso, is also added or is used in place of the sausage. A roux (a mixture of flour and fat) is the traditional thickener, usually augmented with filé powder (ground dried sassafras leaves) or okra. In keeping with today's taste for lighter fare, I swap the smoked sausage and/or ham for my homemade sausage and eliminate the roux. The okra alone does the thickening, and the step of soaking the okra pods in a salt-and-vinegar bath before adding them to the pot ensures they won't be overly viscous. It is important to use dried herbs and canned tomatoes to produce the distinguishing flavors of this dish from a cuisine built around preserved goods. Make sure the okra is fresh, however.

I like to use shrimp in the shell because they enrich the broth. That does make for somewhat messy eating, however. If you want to save your guests the trouble of peeling their own shrimp, remove the shells and simmer them in 1 cup of the broth, then strain the liquid into the pot when adding the remainder of the broth. Shell-on shrimp are easy enough to devein, if it's necessary to do so, by simply cutting through the shell along the back of each shrimp with a sharp paring knife. **SERVES 4**

¼ pound okra, trimmed of tops and cut into ½-inch-thick rounds

2 tablespoons distilled white vinegar

½ teaspoon kosher salt

3 tablespoons extra virgin olive oil

1 yellow or white onion, coarsely chopped

2 ribs celery, coarsely chopped

1 green bell pepper, seeded and coarsely chopped

3 cloves garlic, chopped

1 bay leaf, crumbled

1 teaspoon dried thyme

½ teaspoon dried oregano

¼ teaspoon cayenne pepper

1 cup coarsely chopped canned plum tomatoes, with juice

5 cups chicken broth (page 5)

1 pound Creole Sausage (page 20), formed into 1-inch balls

18 medium-size shrimp, preferably in the shell, deveined if necessary

12 shucked oysters, with liquor

Corn bread for serving (see Skillet Tamale Pie with Mexican Beef Sausage in Jalapeño and Cheese Corn Bread Crust, page 67; made without the sausage)

*continued*

In a medium bowl, toss together the okra, vinegar, and salt. Set aside for about 30 minutes.

Meanwhile, in a large pot, heat 2 tablespoons of the oil over medium heat. Add the onion, celery, bell pepper, and garlic and sauté until well wilted but not browned, about 6 minutes. Stir in the bay leaf, thyme, oregano, cayenne, and tomatoes. Add the broth, raise the heat to medium-high, and bring to a boil. Decrease the heat to maintain a brisk simmer and cook for 30 minutes to blend the flavors.

While the broth simmers, heat the remaining 1 tablespoon oil in a large sauté pan over medium-high heat. Working in batches to avoid crowding, brown the sausage balls on all sides, 7 to 8 minutes per batch. As each batch is finished, transfer the balls to the simmering broth mixture.

When all the balls have been added, rinse the okra and add it to the pot. Continue simmering for 15 minutes. Add the shrimp and the oysters and their liquor, cover the pot, and remove from the heat. Let stand until the shrimp are barely pink and the oysters are slightly plump, about 5 minutes.

Serve right away, accompanied with the corn bread.

# Chorizo

Chorizo, at home in many cuisines, appears with multiple ethnic faces from Spain and Portugal to Mexico, South America, and the Latino-inspired cooking of the American Southwest. It can be stuffed into hog casing and used fresh, or briefly aged in the casing to dry out and intensify the flavors. Sometimes it is smoked, becoming more like a salami in texture. Often it is used fresh in bulk for dishes that benefit from a hit of red and spice. This version comes from Anzonini, a flamenco guitarist and world-class chorizo maker, who generously offered his recipe to Pig-by-the-Tail. We made tons of it, and it was always special! On chorizo-making day, the links were hung on the baking-tray rack for a few hours to dry and compact. The dangling sausages festooned the kitchen like chile-red curtains. It was a spectacle of hospitality and appreciated, judging by the number of customers who came to purchase some to take home when they were "done."

**MAKES 2½ POUNDS**

2 ancho or dried New Mexico red chiles, stems and seeds removed

1 cup water

8 cloves garlic, coarsely chopped

6 ounces salt pork, finely chopped

2½ pounds ground pork

3 tablespoons pure chile powder, preferably ancho

1 teaspoon coarsely ground black pepper

2½ teaspoons kosher salt

In a small saucepan, combine the dried chiles and water and bring to a boil over high heat. Decrease the heat to medium and simmer until the chiles are quite soft, about 5 minutes. Remove from the heat and let cool for 10 minutes.

In a food processor, combine the chiles, 1/4 cup of their cooking water (reserve the remaining water), and the garlic and process to a fine paste. Add the salt pork and process until amalgamated.

Place the ground pork in a large bowl. Add the chile mixture, chile powder, pepper, 2 teaspoons of the salt, and the remaining chile cooking water, and knead with your hands until thoroughly blended. Cook and taste a small sample, then add the remaining 1/2 teaspoon salt, if needed. Leave in bulk and shape as directed in individual recipes or stuff into hog casing. Cover and refrigerate overnight to firm and blend the flavors.

Sauté or grill, or cook as directed in individual recipes. (The uncooked sausage will keep in the refrigerator for up to 5 days, or in the freezer for up to 6 weeks.)

# Black Bean Chili with Chorizo and Chipotle Cream

A glory of black beans, in addition to such qualities as their beauty and healthfulness, is that they don't need to be presoaked: they easily yield to softening when boiled straightaway. Then, they are ready to accept all manner of embellishments, such as sausage, Mexican spices, and sweet-sour-hot chipotle cream. **SERVES 6 TO 8**

**Black Beans**

1½ cups dried black beans

4 cups water

1½ teaspoons kosher salt, or more to taste

**Chili**

2 tablespoons extra virgin olive oil

1 yellow or white onion, chopped

2 large cloves garlic, coarsely chopped

1 pound Chorizo (page 24)

2 teaspoons ground cumin

2 tablespoons pure chile powder, preferably ancho

1 teaspoon chopped fresh oregano or ½ teaspoon dried oregano

1 chipotle chile in adobo sauce, minced

1½ cups canned tomatoes, with juices

4 cups water

**Chipotle Cream**

¾ cup heavy cream

2 tablespoons sour cream

2 chipotle chiles in adobo sauce, minced

To prepare the beans, rinse, pick them over, and place in a large saucepan. Add the water and bring to a boil over high heat. Decrease the heat to maintain a brisk simmer and cook uncovered, adding more water if necessary to keep the beans floating freely, until tender, $1^1/_4$ to $1^1/_2$ hours. Stir in the salt and use right away, or let cool and refrigerate the beans in their cooking liquid for up to 1 week. (The beans can also be cooked in a pressure cooker. Place in the pressure cooker with water to cover by $1^1/_2$ inches, cook for 35 minutes after coming to pressure, and then let stand for 10 minutes to allow the beans to finish cooking as the pressure subsides.)

To make the chili, heat the oil in a large pot over medium-high heat. Add the onion, garlic, chorizo, cumin, chile powder, oregano, and chipotle chile and cook, stirring occasionally to break up the sausage, until the juices are deep red and bubbling, 2 to 3 minutes. Add the black beans and their cooking liquid, the tomatoes, and the water and bring to a boil. Decrease the heat to maintain a brisk simmer and cook, uncovered, until the mixture has a stewlike consistency, about 40 minutes.

While the chili cooks, make the chipotle cream. In a small bowl, whisk together the cream, sour cream, and chiles. Set aside.

To serve, ladle the chili into large bowls, and top each bowl with a dollop of the chipotle cream. Pass the remaining chipotle cream on the side.

# Spanish Egg Cake with Chorizo and Potato

Omelet, frittata, egg tortilla—all are different words for essentially the same thing: eggs mixed with vegetable and/or meat bits and cooked into a cake or pancakelike round. The advantage of this version is that it follows the Spanish or Italian custom of baking the assembled dish. That means no intimidating calisthenics to flip the cake to cook the second side. I serve this informal dish in its cooking skillet, but it's also easy to lift it out onto a platter. **SERVES 4 TO 6**

2 tablespoons extra virgin olive oil

1 or 2 red or Yukon gold potatoes
(½ pound total weight), peeled and
cut into ½-inch dice

¼ cup finely chopped poblano (sometimes
called pasilla) chile

¼ cup finely chopped yellow or white onion

6 ounces Chorizo (page 24)

8 large eggs

1½ teaspoons kosher salt

Preheat the oven to 425°F.

In a 9- to 10-inch skillet, heat the oil over medium-high heat. Add the potato, chile, onion, and chorizo and cook, stirring to break up the sausage, until the vegetables are wilted, 2 to 3 minutes. Remove from the heat.

Break the eggs into a large bowl, add the salt, whisk to mix, and stir in the vegetable-sausage mixture from the skillet. Pour the mixture back into the skillet, place in the oven, and bake until the eggs puff up and a knife inserted in the middle comes out clean, about 10 minutes. Remove from the oven and let cool for 5 minutes or so before serving.

Cut into wedges and serve warm or at room temperature.

# Mexican Meatball Sausage

Mexican meatballs are typically made with a mix of pork and beef (or veal) and include bread crumbs or rice to plump them and egg to bind the ingredients. From there, seasoning variations abound: garlic and/or onion, or not; herbs and/or spices (usually cumin and oregano, sometimes mint); elements such as raisins and/or olives (a Peruvian variation); and so on. Zucchini, the "special ingredient" I use here, was suggested by Mexican cooking maven Diana Kennedy. It lightens and freshens the sausage in a way I find pleasing, so I use it for my basic recipe.

**MAKES 1 POUND**

½ pound ground pork

½ pound ground beef

½ cup fresh bread crumbs (page 4)

3 cups grated zucchini, grated on the
    medium-size holes of a box grater

1 teaspoon ground cumin

½ teaspoon dried oregano

1 teaspoon kosher salt

¼ teaspoon freshly ground black pepper

1 large egg

Place all the ingredients in a medium bowl, and knead with your hands until thoroughly blended. Cover and refrigerate for at least 1 hour or up to overnight to firm the sausage and blend the flavors.

Form into balls and cook as directed in individual recipes. (The uncooked sausage will keep in the refrigerator for up to 3 days, or in the freezer for up to 1 week.)

# Mexican Meatballs in Toasted Garlic–Ancho Chile Broth

In many Mexican marketplaces and town plazas, the aroma of garlic soup wafts from nearby restaurants, beckoning as you shop, promenade, or just wander and gawk. It's an ancient soup, dating from the time the Moors introduced a brothy concoction to the Iberian Peninsula, which the locals thickened with pulverized almonds (Chicken and Almond Meatballs in White Gazpacho, page 115). In the New World, the soup was re-created to include tomatoes and dried chiles. That rendition came to be embraced by lovers of Latin fare from the coast of Spain to the zocalos of Mexican towns to the American cities of the Pacific coast. It is an ardently delicious, deep red, beautiful soup that brings with it a blessing of health to the diners, and is blessedly easy to make. **SERVES 4 TO 6**

1 pound Mexican Meatball Sausage (page 27), formed into walnut-size balls

2 large dried red chiles, preferably ancho

7 cups water

¼ cup extra virgin olive oil, plus more as needed

10 cloves garlic, coarsely chopped

12 baguette slices, ½ inch thick

1 cup canned tomato sauce

¾ teaspoon kosher salt

2 tablespoons heavy cream, whipped until thick

First, make the meatballs and set them aside in the refrigerator.

To prepare the chiles, stem them and shake out the seeds, leaving the pods more or less whole. In a small saucepan, combine the chile pods and 2 cups of the water and bring to a boil over medium-high heat. Cover and simmer until plumped up and soft, about 5 minutes. Remove from the heat and let cool until the chiles can be handled. Lift out the pods and reserve the water. Slit open each chile, scrape the pulp off the skin, and discard the skin. Add the pulp to the reserved water and set aside.

To make the soup, heat the ¼ cup oil in a large sauté pan over medium heat. Add the garlic and cook, stirring, until beginning to turn golden, about 1 minute. With a slotted spoon, transfer to a large pot. Working in batches to avoid crowding, toast the bread slices in the same sauté pan, turning and adding more oil as necessary to keep them from being dry toasted, until lightly golden on both sides, 1 to 2 minutes for each batch. Transfer to paper towels to drain. When all the bread is toasted, set the slices aside.

*continued*

Again working in batches to avoid crowding, brown the meatballs in the same pan over medium-high heat, adding oil as needed, until golden all around, about 5 minutes. Transfer to the pot with the garlic as you go. Add the tomato sauce, the remaining 5 cups water, the salt, and the reserved cooking water with the chile pulp to the pot and bring to a boil over high heat. Decrease the heat to maintain a brisk simmer, partially cover the pot, and cook until the garlic is soft and the meatballs are tender, about 20 minutes.

To serve, ladle the soup into individual bowls. Garnish each bowl with 2 or 3 toasted bread slices and a dollop of the cream.

# Mexican Meatballs Simmered in Tomatillo Sauce with Black Olives

Tomatillos are a member of the nightshade family, which includes New World tomatoes and potatoes and such Old World relatives as eggplants. Although those wide-ranging kin have become familiar around the globe, tomatillos remain something of a country cousin, not much appreciated or grown outside Mexico and its neighbors to the south in Central and South America and to the north in California and the American Southwest. Tomatillos are an everyday must in Mexican cooking and dining, however, especially for one of Mexico's great table sauces, *salsa verde*. Here the sauce, usually used as a dip for tortilla chips, becomes the medium for simmering meatballs. Make this recipe in summer, when tomatillos are in season. Canned versions are available, but they should be reserved for thickening *chile verde* and the like, much as okra is used in southern cooking. **SERVES 4**

**Salsa**

10 ounces tomatillos, husks removed

¼ small white or yellow onion, coarsely chopped

1½ cups water

2 jalapeño chiles, coarsely cut up

2 cups fresh cilantro leaves and tender stems

Kosher salt

2 tablespoons butter or ghee (see page 71)

1 pound Mexican Meatball Sausage (page 27), formed into walnut-size balls

16 Kalamata olives, pitted and coarsely chopped

About 16 fresh cilantro sprigs

½ teaspoon cider vinegar or fresh lime juice

Pinch of kosher salt

To make the salsa, combine the tomatillos, onion, and water in a medium saucepan and bring to a boil over high heat. Remove from the heat, cover, and let stand until the tomatillos are soft enough to pierce easily but have not collapsed, 8 to 10 minutes. Uncover, let cool slightly, then transfer the tomatillos, onion, and ½ cup of the cooking water to a food processor. Add the chiles, cilantro, and ½ teaspoon salt and process until almost smooth. Taste and adjust the salt. Use right away, or cover and refrigerate for up to 3 days.

Place a heavy sauté pan large enough to hold the meatballs without crowding over medium-high heat and melt the butter. Add the meatballs and sauté until browned all around, 3 to 5 minutes. Stir in the salsa and olives, decrease the heat to maintain a gentle simmer, cover, and cook until the meatballs are tender and the sauce is thickened, 10 to 12 minutes.

To serve, in a small bowl, toss the cilantro sprigs with the vinegar and salt. Transfer the meatballs and their sauce to a serving dish and strew the dressed sprigs over the top. Serve right away.

# Toulouse Sausage

I opened Pig-by-the-Tail because I wanted to bring to the American marketplace the charcuterie I had fallen in love with on sojourns to France, Spain, Italy, Germany, and Austria. Two years after its debut, I decided it was time to put some "bones" onto that passion. I traveled to France to learn from M. Roger Gleize, the charcutier in the small town of Revel in the Haute-Garonne just outside of Toulouse. It was an eye-opening experience to watch him use a hand grinder to grind pounds and pounds of perfectly succulent pork, not too lean, not too fat, for the region's specialty Toulouse sausage. He seasoned the meat with salt, peppers, and a dash each of nutmeg and sugar, and then added a soupçon of water to moisten the mixture for easier stuffing. He fitted the same manual machine with a sausage-stuffing funnel and proceeded to turn out a seemingly endless supply of fresh Toulouse sausages. Everything he made was quickly purchased by local households to use for their daily meals and by local restaurants to include in the renowned cassoulet of the region.

From that sojourn, I carried home a deep admiration for simply, yet perfectly done ways with food, and Toulouse sausage became one of my go-to household sausages. For this book, I have modified the recipe to call for bulk sausage, rather than links. But, if you would like to follow tradition, use hog casing. **MAKES 2 ¼ POUNDS**

2 pounds ground pork

¼ pound salt pork, fat only, minced

½ teaspoon freshly ground black pepper

1 teaspoon freshly ground white pepper

¼ teaspoon freshly grated nutmeg

1½ teaspoons sugar

1½ teaspoons kosher salt, or to taste, if needed

¼ cup water

Place the pork, salt pork, black pepper, white pepper, nutmeg, sugar, and salt in a large bowl and mix with your hands to distribute the seasonings evenly. Add the water and continue mixing with your hands until the ingredients are thoroughly blended. Cook and taste a small sample, then add more salt if needed. Leave in bulk and shape as directed in individual recipes or stuff into hog casing. Cover and refrigerate for 1 hour to firm.

Sauté or grill, or cook as directed in individual recipes. (The uncooked sausage will keep in the refrigerator for up to 3 days, or in the freezer for up to 1 week.)

# Lunch Pie, aka Quiche, with Toulouse Sausage and Spinach

In the 1970s, when everyone and their sisters and brothers became enchanted with French cooking, with Julia Child leading the way, quiche became *the* savory custard pie. The classic, quiche Lorraine, made with bacon and Gruyère cheese to enrich the custard, enjoyed star status as an elegant staple for brunch or for a first course in a multitiered dinner à la français. Variations in great numbers soon followed, and quiche in one or another guise turned into a favorite on buffet tables and appetizer menus. Here, with Toulouse sausage and a green splotch of spinach, the lovable custard-in-a-crust reinvents itself into an uncomplicated light dinner.

Even though it is easier to purchase a prepared pastry crust, to settle for that is to miss the flaky, unctuous mouth delight of a homemade one. A food processor provides a quick, simple, and almost hands-free way to make an exceptional crust. A removable-bottom tart pan, such as the type the French would use for quiche and sweet dessert tarts, makes it easy to present the pie standing alone rather than in a dish, which is more awkward to serve from.

**MAKES ONE 9- TO 10-INCH PIE, SERVES 4 TO 6**

**Crust**

1¼ cups all-purpose flour, plus more for rolling

Pinch of salt

½ cup (1 stick) cold unsalted butter

2 tablespoons chilled water

**Filling**

2 cups packed coarsely chopped fresh spinach leaves

Extra virgin olive oil, for cooking

¼ pound Toulouse Sausage (page 32), crumbled

2 large eggs

¾ cup heavy cream

½ teaspoon kosher salt

Pinch of freshly grated nutmeg

Pinch of cayenne paper

2 cups coarsely grated melting cheese, such as Gruyère, Emmentaler, Fontina, or Monterey jack

To make the crust, place the 1¼ cups of flour and salt in a food processor and pulse once to mix. Cut the butter into ½-inch pieces and scatter over the flour. Pulse until the mixture is somewhat crumbly. Add the water and pulse again until the mixture adheres when squeezed between your fingers. Gather the dough into a loose ball and wrap in plastic wrap. Press into a smooth disk and refrigerate for at least 30 minutes, or up to 2 days. Bring to room temperature before using.

*continued*

Preheat the oven to 400°F.

On a lightly floured work surface, roll out the dough into a round about 2 inches larger than a 9- to 10-inch tart pan. Transfer the round to the pan, easing it into the bottom and up the sides. Fold in any excess dough hanging above the top and press it against the pan so it adheres. Prick the crust all across the bottom with a fork.

Bake until barely golden on the bottom and around the edges, about 25 minutes. Remove from the oven and set aside, leaving the oven on.

To make the filling, rinse the spinach and shake off the excess water, leaving the spinach slightly moist. Place in a microwave-safe bowl or in a sauté pan. Cover and place in the microwave oven, or cover and cook on the stove top over medium heat until wilted but still bright green, 1 to 2 minutes by either method. Let cool, squeeze out the remaining moisture, and set aside.

Add just enough oil to a small sauté pan to film the bottom and place over medium-high heat. Add the sausage and cook, stirring to break up the clumps, until beginning to brown, 2 to 3 minutes.Remove from the heat, and spread the sausage across the bottom of the partially baked crust.

Combine the eggs, cream, salt, nutmeg, and cayenne in a medium bowl and whisk to blend. Whisk in the cheese and stir in the spinach. Pour the custard mixture into the crust.

Bake until the filling puffs up and is golden on top and a fork inserted in the center comes out clean but still a little moist, about 30 minutes. Serve warm or at room temperature.

# Toulouse Sausage–Stuffed Duck Legs with White Beans

On my brief sojourn in the Toulouse area, I traveled to many local villages and towns acclaimed for their charcuterie. Among them was Castelnaudary, a small village built of stone, close by the fairy-tale-like medieval castle of Carcassonne. The castle was a thrill; even more so was the cassoulet I enjoyed in Castelnaudary, known as the cradle of cassoulet. I mustered the nerve to ask the chef what his secret was. He graciously shared his version of "the cassoulet secret": The kind of beans you use is crucial. They should be lingot beans, also called white kidney beans or cannellini beans, or coco beans, which resemble slightly elongated navy beans. Both are sweetly buttery and cook up soft and tender enough to soak up juices, but still hold their shape. Then, the beans must be allowed to cool completely in their cooking liquid before assembling the cassoulet. Overnight is best.

Stuffed whole duck legs (drumstick and thigh combination) make a delectable sausage star for a faux cassoulet. To sidestep the lengthy process of curing the duck overnight then braising it in duck fat to make confit, the whole legs are sprinkled with a salt and herb seasoning and refrigerated for a few hours to allow the seasonings to imbue. The sausage is then stuffed under the thigh skin, making a single package of sausage and duck meat. **SERVES 6**

1½ teaspoons coarse sea salt

6 fresh thyme sprigs or 1 teaspoon dried thyme

¾ teaspoon juniper berries, crushed

¾ teaspoon coarsely ground black pepper

6 whole duck legs, 7 to 8 ounces each

2½ cups dried cannellini, coco, or Great Northern beans

1 teaspoon kosher salt

¾ pound Toulouse Sausage (page 32)

1 tablespoon extra virgin olive oil or duck fat

3 cups chicken broth (page 5)

1 tablespoon tomato paste

2 cups fresh bread crumbs (page 4)

To prepare the duck, mix together the coarse salt, thyme, juniper, and pepper in a small bowl. Place the duck pieces in a nonreactive container large enough to hold them in a single, tightly packed layer. Spread the salt mixture over the duck and turn the duck to coat on both sides. Loosely cover with plastic wrap, place a weight of some sort on top, and refrigerate for 3 or 4 hours.

*continued*

To prepare the beans, first presoak them using the quick-soak method: Place in a large pot with water to cover generously and bring to a boil over high heat. Remove from the heat and let stand for 1 to 2 hours. To cook the beans, drain and rinse them and return them to the pot. Add water to cover generously and bring to a boil over high heat. Decrease the heat to maintain a brisk simmer and cook, uncovered, until the beans are tender, about 2 hours. (The beans can also be cooked in a pressure cooker without presoaking. Place in the pressure cooker with water to cover by $1^1/_2$ inches, cook for 35 to 40 minutes after coming to pressure, then let stand for 10 minutes to allow the beans to finish cooking as the pressure subsides.) Stir in the kosher salt, and let cool completely in the liquid, preferably overnight, in the refrigerator.

When ready to cook the cassoulet, preheat the oven to 350°F.

Rinse the duck legs and pat them dry. Using your fingers and a paring knife, lift up the thigh skin on each leg and stuff the sausage between the skin and meat, dividing the sausage evenly among the legs.

In a large sauté pan, heat the oil over medium-high heat. Working in batches if necessary to avoid crowding, add the duck legs, skin side down, and cook, turning once, until browned on both sides, about 6 minutes total. Transfer to a plate.

Drain the cooled beans and transfer them to a baking dish large enough to hold the duck pieces in a single, tightly packed layer. Add the broth and tomato paste to the beans and stir to mix. Set the duck pieces on the beans, cover the dish, and bake until the juices are bubbling and the duck is beginning to turn golden around the edges, 30 to 40 minutes.

Uncover the dish and sprinkle the bread crumbs evenly across the top. Continue baking, uncovered, until the duck is golden on top and the bread crumbs are well toasted, 15 to 20 minutes. If the crumbs start to burn, ladle some of the juice from the dish over them. Serve piping hot.

# Sweet Italian Sausage

The fennel-spiked sausage that turns up in such favorite Italian American preparations as pizza, meatball sandwiches (page 38), custardy casseroles, and savory pies has so captured the heart of American cooking that it can be found in supermarkets and deli cases from the Atlantic seaboard to the Pacific Northwest and everywhere in between. Not only is it one of the tastiest and most popular sausages, but it is also one of the easiest to make at home because it doesn't require a casing. In fact, most recipes call for taking it out of its casing. If you want to serve the sausage as links, stuff it into hog casing. The recipe yields a larger amount than the other recipes in the book because this sausage is so versatile that I like to have some on hand in the freezer.

**MAKES 2 POUNDS**

1¾ pounds ground pork

¼ pound salt pork, fat part only, minced

2 cloves garlic, minced or pressed

1 teaspoon chopped fresh oregano or scant
½ teaspoon dried oregano

1 teaspoon chopped fresh thyme or scant
½ teaspoon dried thyme

2 teaspoons fennel seeds

½ teaspoon freshly ground black pepper

⅛ teaspoon cayenne pepper

½ cup white wine

1 teaspoon kosher salt, or to taste, if needed

Place all the ingredients except the salt in a large bowl, and knead with your hands until thoroughly blended. Cook and taste a small sample, then add the salt if needed. Leave in bulk and shape as directed in individual recipes or stuff into hog casing. Cover and refrigerate for several hours, or preferably overnight, to allow the flavors to blend.

Sauté or grill, or cook as directed in individual recipes. (The uncooked sausage will keep in the refrigerator for up to 3 days, or in the freezer for up to 1 week.)

# Pittsburgh-Style Sausage Sandwich with Chunky Tomato and Bell Pepper Sauce

Why Pittsburgh? Because James Potenziani, known to all as "Chooch," is Italian American and grew up in Pittsburgh. He was the master behind the sausage machine at Pig-by-the-Tail. He is also a football person (he always roots for the Steelers), and he devised the Pittsburgh sausage sandwich to celebrate on Super Bowl day. It became a year-round favorite at Pig-by-the-Tail.

**SERVES 6 TO 8**

**Sauce**

⅓ cup extra virgin olive oil

2 yellow or white onions, halved lengthwise and cut into ½-inch-wide strips

2 cloves garlic, finely chopped

3 green bell peppers, halved lengthwise, seeded, and cut lengthwise into ½-inch-wide strips

2 small red or green chiles, finely chopped

1 tablespoon chopped fresh oregano, or 1½ teaspoons dried oregano

2 pounds fresh tomatoes, chopped, or 3 cups canned plum tomatoes, chopped, with juices

Kosher salt

¾ teaspoon freshly ground black pepper

Extra virgin olive oil, for cooking

2 pounds Sweet Italian Sausage (page 37), formed into 1¼-inch balls

6 to 8 Italian or French bread rolls, or 2 baguettes

To make the sauce, heat the oil in a large sauté pan over medium heat. Add the onions, garlic, bell peppers, chiles, and oregano and sauté until the onions and peppers have softened but not browned, about 5 minutes. Add the tomatoes and their juices, salt to taste, and the pepper, decrease the heat to maintain a brisk simmer, and cook, uncovered, until thickened, about 45 minutes.

Meanwhile, brown the meatballs. Add just enough oil to a large sauté pan to film the bottom and place over medium-high heat. Working in batches to avoid crowding, add the sausage balls and brown all around, about 10 minutes. As each batch is done, transfer to a plate.

When the sauce is ready, add the browned sausage balls and continue cooking until the sauce is reduced and the sausages are cooked through and tender, about 20 minutes.

To serve, split the rolls lengthwise. Or, if using baguettes, cut each baguette crosswise into thirds or quarters, and then split the sections lengthwise. Place the bottom halves of the rolls, cut sides up, on individual plates. Divide the sausage balls evenly among the roll bottoms and spoon plenty of sauce over the top. Close the sandwiches and serve right away with lots of napkins.

# Bread Pizza with Fried Egg and Sausage

When I was growing up, fried egg sandwiches were one of my mother's specialties, and we often had them for lunch on weekends. The sandwiches were made in her New Mexico cooking style: The eggs were turned once and fried until the whites were crisp around the edges and the yolks were well set. Then they were transferred to slices of white bread that had been slathered with mayonnaise, and a lettuce leaf was slipped between the egg and the bread. Here's my contemporary version of that homey sandwich. Its siren call of melted, oozing cheese and added bonus of sausage bits turn my mom's simpler lunchtime sandwich into a mini-meal on bread. In keeping with the pizza theme, I call for sweet Italian or Tuscan sausage. But American Breakfast Sausage (page 10) or Spicy Garlic Sausage (page 48) would also do nicely. **SERVES 6**

Extra virgin olive oil, for cooking and
   brushing on bread

½ pound Sweet Italian Sausage (page 37)
   or Tuscan Sausage (page 41)

2 tablespoons butter

6 large eggs

1 (1-pound) loaf *ciabatta* or other rustic
   Italian bread

6 ounces Monterey jack cheese, coarsely
   grated

¼ teaspoon chile flakes

6 thin tomato slices, cut in half

Preheat the oven to 350°F.

Add just enough oil to a large sauté pan to film the bottom and place over medium heat. Crumble the sausage into chunks and add it to the pan. Cook until lightly browned, 2 to 3 minutes. Transfer the sausage to a plate and set aside in a warm place.

In the same pan, melt the butter over medium-high heat. Crack the eggs into the pan and cook until the whites are firm, about 5 minutes, or until done as you like. Set the pan aside in a warm place with the eggs still in it.

Cut the bread loaf crosswise into thirds, then split each section lengthwise. Place, cut sides up, on a rimmed baking sheet. Lightly brush the cut sides of the bread with oil, then divide the cheese evenly among them. Sprinkle the chile flakes over the cheese, arrange the tomato slices on the cheese, and then top evenly with the sausage.

Bake until the cheese melts and the bread begins to turn golden around the edges, 7 to 8 minutes.

Place a fried egg atop each "pizza" and serve right away.

# Tuscan Sausage

There's almost no turn in Tuscany that doesn't provide some sensory joy. Driving its curvy roads through low hills gently swelling up from narrow, verdant valleys, you discover olive groves that produce some of the world's finest olive oil and vineyards that yield some of the world's most renowned wines. Exploring the region's old towns and cities on foot, you wind your way through dozens of museums full of famous artworks and wander into back-alley churches and quaint shops stacked with Tuscan treasures. And everywhere, there is fabulous food. The Tuscans have long produced delicious *salumi*, that special form of pork cookery, called *charcuterie* in France, that comprises prosciutto, mortadella, *soppressata*, salamis and other cured meats, along with fresh sausages particular to the region. In this recipe, sun-dried tomatoes, basil, and mozzarella flavor fresh pork sausage to deliver the taste of Tuscany.

**MAKES 1 POUND**

14 ounces ground pork

2 ounces salt pork, fat part only, minced

¼ cup finely chopped unseasoned olive oil–packed sun-dried tomatoes

⅓ cup lightly packed coarsely grated mozzarella cheese (about 2 ounces)

1 small clove garlic, minced or pressed

3 teaspoons chopped fresh basil leaves

2 teaspoons chopped fresh flat-leaf parsley leaves

½ teaspoon freshly ground black pepper

1 teaspoon kosher salt, or to taste, if needed

Place all the ingredients except the salt in a medium bowl, and knead with your hands until thoroughly blended. Cook and taste a small sample, then add the salt if needed. Leave in bulk and shape as directed in individual recipes or stuff into hog casing. Cover and refrigerate for at least 4 hours before using to allow the flavors to blend.

Sauté or grill, or cook as directed in individual recipes. (The uncooked sausage will keep in the refrigerator for up to 3 days; it does not freeze well.)

# Minestrone Soup with Tuscan Sausage and Arugula Pesto

Minestrone has a long history in Italian cuisine and, not surprisingly, many interpretations. Old tales recount how Roman soldiers lived on a diet of minestrone and chickpeas, a strange assertion since many of the soup's classic ingredients—tomatoes, potatoes, beans—are New World foods that were not available at the time. By the end of the sixteenth century, the core concept had become a tasty mixture of vegetables, including dried beans, with pasta and/or potatoes. If you can find them, use borlotti (cranberry) beans, a specialty of Tuscany.

Swirling a pesto of arugula, rather than the more prosaic basil, into the minestrone imparts a refreshing change. Other unusual elements in the soup are a tiny spritz of vinegar and the use of shallot instead of garlic. The pesto is also good for dolloping on plain boiled potatoes or a simply cooked fish fillet or chicken breast, or on bruschetta, for serving as an appetizer. **SERVES 6**

## Pesto

½ cup pine nuts

1 large shallot, cut up

2 cups packed arugula leaves

1 cup fresh flat-leaf parsley leaves

¾ teaspoon kosher salt, or more to taste

1½ teaspoons red wine vinegar

½ cup extra virgin olive oil

½ cup freshly grated Parmesan cheese

## Soup

2 tablespoons extra virgin olive oil

1 yellow or white onion, finely chopped

1 large clove garlic, finely chopped

1 small carrot, coarsely chopped

1 rib celery, coarsely chopped

½ teaspoon chopped fresh oregano or ¼ teaspoon dried oregano

¼ teaspoon chopped fresh rosemary

2 teaspoons kosher salt

2 tablespoons tomato paste

5 cups chicken broth (page 5)

5 cups water

1½ cups cooked dried beans, such as borlotti, cannellini, or Great Northern

1 large waxy potato, such as red, white, or Yukon gold, peeled and cut into neat ½-inch cubes

1 pound Tuscan Sausage (page 41), formed into cherry tomato–size balls

To make the pesto, in a food processor, combine the pine nuts and shallot and process until very finely chopped. Add the remaining ingredients and process until the mixture is as smooth as possible. Set aside, or cover and refrigerate for up to 3 days.

To make the soup, in a large pot, heat the oil over medium heat. Add the onion and garlic and sauté until wilted, 2 minutes. Add the carrot, celery, oregano, rosemary, and salt and sauté until the vegetables are slightly softened, about 5 minutes.

Stir in the tomato paste, broth, and water, raise the heat to medium-high, and bring to a boil. Decrease the heat to maintain a gentle simmer and cook, uncovered, until the vegetables are tender and the broth is richly flavored, about 15 minutes.

Add the potato and sausage balls and continue cooking, uncovered, until the potatoes are just soft enough to mash, 20 to 25 minutes.

To serve, ladle the soup into individual bowls. Top each bowl with 1 tablespoon or so of the pesto. Pass the remaining pesto at the table.

# Fresh Polish Sausage

The familiar Polish sausage known as kielbasa was introduced to American cuisine in the neighborhoods of Chicago, New York, New Jersey, Pennsylvania, and Michigan, where many Polish immigrants settled during the late nineteenth and early twentieth centuries. Nowadays, kielbasa is widely produced commercially and is marketed to food purveyors nationwide. It is usually smoked and sandwiched in a hot dog bun, tucked into a hearty cabbage borscht, or added to a robust sauerkraut dish (page 46). That is not the whole story, however. Kielbasa is actually the generic term for sausage in Polish and there are many versions. I prefer a fresh, not smoked, sausage, but with a hint of ham to suggest a smoky flavor. **MAKES 1 POUND**

½ pound ground pork

6 ounces ground beef or veal

1 ounce mild ham, minced

1 ounce salt pork, minced

1 small clove garlic, minced or pressed

1 teaspoon dried marjoram

½ teaspoon dry mustard

½ teaspoon sugar

1 teaspoon kosher salt, or to taste, if needed

¼ teaspoon freshly ground black pepper

½ cup full-flavored beer (not dark beer)

Place all the ingredients in a bowl, and knead with your hands until thoroughly blended and no longer wet. Cook and taste a small sample, then add more salt if needed. Leave in bulk and shape as directed in individual recipes, stuff into hog casing, or wrap in cheesecloth if using for Honey-Glazed Polish Sausage (page 45).

Sauté or grill, or cook as directed in individual recipes. (The uncooked sausage will keep in the refrigerator for up to 3 days, or in the freezer for up to 1 week.)

# Honey-Glazed Fresh Polish Sausage with Sautéed Apples

One morning, Penny Brogden, my longtime friend and coworker at Pig-by-the Tail, came dancing into the kitchen, exclaiming, "I did the Polish sausages for dinner last night the best way ever! I glazed them with honey and baked them." We tried the same preparation on the spot, and she was right. It was a fabulous way to give the ordinary a new polish. We advised customers who purchased Polish sausage to make the dish, too, and it was included in *American Charcuterie*, my book of recipes from Pig-by-the-Tail. If you are not set up for stuffing the sausage into hog casing, form it into links, wrap the links in cheesecloth, and refrigerate overnight (see page 154).

**SERVES 4 TO 6**

2 pounds Fresh Polish Sausage (page 44), preferably in links

½ cup aromatic honey, such as orange blossom or thyme flower

3 tablespoons butter

4 large sweet-tart apples such as Fuji or Braeburn (see page 102), unpeeled, halved, cored, and cut into1-inch wedges

Preheat the oven to 350°F.

To cook the sausages, bring a large pot of water to a boil. Add the sausages (don't unwrap them if they are in cheesecloth) and parboil until firm, 5 minutes. Drain and set aside to cool. Unwrap the cheesecloth and place the sausages side by side in a baking dish. Pour the honey over them and turn to coat all around. Place in the oven and bake, basting two or three times, until bronze colored, 15 to 20 minutes.

Meanwhile, cook the apples. In a large sauté pan, melt the butter over medium-low heat. Add the apples and cook, turning often, until deep gold on the outside and soft all the way through, 30 minutes or so, depending on the size of the pan and the type of apple.

Transfer the sausages and apples to a platter and serve.

# Fresh Polish Sausage Braised in Sauerkraut with Parsleyed Potatoes

An unassuming regional dish of sauerkraut with various charcuterie meats—sausage, duck confit, salt pork—garnered three stars for the restaurant L'Auberge de l'Ill, located on the banks of the River Ill in picturesque Alsace, and made both the specialty, *choucroute garnie*, and the restaurant classics in the world of European haute cuisine. It's one of my favorite composed pork dishes, and I often cook a simple but still lusty version of it with robust Polish sausage. If you'd like to make it more elaborate, add baby back ribs baked until half done and/or the cured duck legs without the Toulouse sausage stuffing (page 35) to the sauerkraut.

The juniper berries lend a clear, piney fragrance. If you don't have any on hand, 1 tablespoon of good gin, the spirit they flavor, can be substituted. **SERVES 6**

**Sauerkraut**

4 tablespoons butter

4 ounces salt pork, preferably with rind, cut into ½-by-1-inch pieces

2 yellow or white onions, halved and sliced ⅛ inch thick

¾ teaspoon caraway seeds

½ teaspoon black peppercorns, crushed with a mallet

10 juniper berries, crushed

1½ teaspoons chopped fresh thyme or ¾ teaspoon dried thyme

3 pounds sauerkraut, drained and lightly squeezed

1 cup white wine

1 cup chicken broth (page 5)

1 pound Fresh Polish Sausage (page 44), stuffed in hog casing or hand formed into links about 3½ inches long by 1 inch in diameter

**Potatoes**

2 pounds red or Yukon gold potatoes, peeled and cut into ½-inch chunks

Kosher salt

3 tablespoons butter

¼ cup chopped fresh flat-leaf parsley

Preheat the oven to 350°F.

To make the sauerkraut, melt 2 tablespoons of the butter in a large sauté pan over medium heat. Add the salt pork and sauté until barely beginning to turn golden, 4 to 5 minutes. Add the onions, stir to coat them well, and sauté until they are softened but not browned, about 6 minutes. Stir in the caraway, peppercorns, juniper, thyme, and sauerkraut, mixing with a fork to separate the sauerkraut strands. Add the wine and broth and bring to a boil over high heat. Transfer the contents of the sauté pan to a large ovensafe pan or clay pot, cover, and bake, stirring once or twice, until lightly brown around the edges, about 1 hour.

Meanwhile, in the same sauté pan used for the onions, melt the remaining 2 tablespoons butter over medium heat. Add the sausages and sauté until golden all around, 4 to 5 minutes. Set aside.

When the sauerkraut has cooked for 1 hour, add the sausages, pressing them in so they are well embedded. Decrease the oven heat to 325°F, cover, and continue cooking until most of the liquid has evaporated, about 30 minutes.

While the sauerkraut and sausages finish cooking, prepare the potatoes. Place them in a large pot, add water to cover generously and a teaspoon or so of salt, and bring to a boil over high heat. Decrease the heat to maintain a brisk simmer and cook until they can be pierced all the way through, 10 to 15 minutes. Drain the potatoes, return them to the pot, and add the butter and parsley. Without stirring, cover the pot and set aside in a warm place.

To serve, present the sauerkraut in the clay pot, if you used one, or spoon it onto a platter. Gently stir the potatoes, season them with salt, and serve them in a separate bowl on the side.

# Spicy Garlic Sausage

Herbaceous and zesty, this sausage is an excellent all-purpose choice for whenever you want to add a sausage element that is neither too strident nor too wimpy. I especially like it for the vindaloo on page 49, where it stands up to the other forceful seasonings in the dish.

**MAKES 1½ POUNDS**

1¼ pounds ground pork

2 ounces salt pork, fat only, minced

2 teaspoons minced jalapeño chile

1 clove garlic, minced or pressed

½ teaspoon finely chopped fresh sage or
   ¼ teaspoon dried sage

1 tablespoon chopped fresh flat-leaf parsley

¼ teaspoon freshly ground black pepper

Pinch of cayenne pepper

⅓ cup red wine

1 teaspoon kosher salt, or to taste, if needed

Place all the ingredients except the salt in a medium bowl, and knead with your hands until thoroughly blended. Cook and taste a small sample, then add the salt if needed. Leave in bulk and shape as directed in individual recipes or stuff into hog casing. Cover and refrigerate for at least 4 hours, or preferably overnight, to firm and to blend the flavors.

Sauté or grill, or cook as directed in individual recipes. (The uncooked sausage will keep in the refrigerator for up to 5 days, or in the freezer for up to 3 weeks.)

# Spicy Garlic Sausage Vindaloo with Dried Plum Chutney

Vindaloo originated in the tiny state of Goa, on India's southwest coast, which was colonized by the Portuguese in the sixteenth century. Because the Portuguese are traditionally Christian, pork is not proscribed in Goa, as it is almost everywhere else in India. Vindaloo, however, has been embraced throughout India and beyond, reinterpreted sometimes with chicken, sometimes with beef or lamb, so that it can be enjoyed within religious bounds. In fact, vindaloo with any meat, or even as a vegetarian dish, has an irresistible sweet-salty-sour-hot flavor. And though it seems intimidatingly spicy at first, one taste and you are hooked.

A fruit chutney, to both soothe and stimulate the palate, is an expected complement for many Indian meals. Here, dried plums fit that bill in a chutney that can be enjoyed year-round not only with this dish, but with nearly any pork, poultry, or game dish, as well.

I won't tell you any lies: this dish is for a day when you feel like cooking. The good news is that it is a one-pot meal and worth it. **SERVES 6 TO 8**

### Chutney

1 cup dried plums, cut lengthwise into quarters

¼ red onion, cut in half lengthwise and cut crosswise into ¼-inch-thick slices

1 tablespoon coarsely chopped orange peel (not just the zest)

1 tablespoon fresh orange juice

1 tablespoon balsamic vinegar

2 tablespoons packed light or dark brown sugar

Small pinch of cardamom seeds

Small pinch of cayenne pepper

1 cup cold water

### Vindaloo

3 yellow or white onions, 1 coarsely chopped, 2 quartered and thinly sliced

6 cloves garlic, coarsely chopped

2 tablespoons peeled and coarsely chopped fresh ginger

2 teaspoons ground cumin

¼ teaspoon ground cinnamon

¼ teaspoon ground cloves

2 tablespoons cider vinegar

1½ pounds Spicy Garlic Sausage (page 48), formed into 1-inch balls

2 tablespoons peanut or canola oil

2 teaspoons yellow mustard seeds

6 small dried red chiles, such as cayenne or japones, broken into pieces

1½-inch piece tamarind pulp

2 cups warm water

4 tablespoons butter

2 teaspoons ground turmeric

1½ teaspoons pure chile powder, preferably ancho or New Mexico

1 teaspoon kosher salt

3 waxy potatoes, such as Yukon gold, red, or white, peeled and cut into 1-inch cubes

2 cups plain yogurt, whisked smooth

*continued*

To make the chutney, combine all the ingredients in a small saucepan and toss to mix. Place over medium heat, bring to a simmer, cover, and cook until the liquid is almost gone, 8 to 10 minutes. Or, combine the ingredients in a microwave-safe bowl and microwave for 8 to 10 minutes. Set the chutney aside, or cool, cover, and refrigerate for up to 1 month.

To make the vindaloo, combine the chopped onion, garlic, ginger, cumin, cinnamon, cloves, and cider vinegar in a food processor and process until as smooth as possible. Transfer to a large bowl, add the sausage balls, and turn gently to coat evenly. Cover and place in the refrigerator to marinate while preparing the rest of the ingredients, or for up to overnight.

When ready to cook, heat the oil over medium-high heat in a small, heavy saucepan. Add the mustard seeds and chiles and sauté until the mustard seeds begin to pop, 3 to 4 minutes. Remove from the heat and set aside.

In a small bowl, soften the tamarind pulp in the warm water for about 30 minutes. Pour into a fine-mesh sieve set over a bowl to capture the liquid, pressing down on the pulp to extract as much liquid as possible. Set aside.

When ready to cook the dish, melt the butter in a large enameled pot over medium heat. Add the sliced onions, stir to coat with the butter, and cook gently until soft and beginning to turn golden, 15 to 20 minutes.

Add the meatballs and their paste, the turmeric, chile powder, salt, and tamarind liquid and bring to a boil over medium heat, turning the sausage balls as needed to coat evenly. Cover partially, adjust the heat to maintain a gentle simmer, and cook until the sausage balls are almost cooked but are still pink in the center, about 20 minutes.

Gently stir the potatoes into the pot and continue cooking, partially covered, until the potatoes are easily pierced all the way through, 15 to 20 minutes longer.

Transfer the vindaloo to a serving dish. Serve right away with the yogurt and dried plum chutney on the side.

# Spicy Garlic Sausage with French Lentils and Chicory

In a showcase dish for slow-cooking-meets-quick-and-easy, sausage and lentils come together in a hearty combination for cool weather. The slow part is making the sausage, which is actually a cinch and can be done days in advance. The quick-and-easy part is that the dish cooks in about half an hour. Of all the many, many kinds of lentils, which vary in size, color, and their use in cooking, French green lentils are perfect for preparations such as this one where you want the lentils to cook up soft to the center while retaining their shape and not collapsing into a puree, as would be desirable, for instance, in an Indian dal. The soupçon of balsamic vinegar is stirred in just before serving so its tang and aroma remain bright and boldly present, not faded into the background. **SERVES 6 TO 8**

2 tablespoons extra virgin olive oil

1½ pounds Spicy Garlic Sausage (page 48), formed into 1-inch balls

1 medium yellow or white onion, finely chopped

1 medium carrot, peeled and finely chopped

1 large clove garlic, finely chopped

1 small bay leaf, crumbled

1 teaspoon chopped fresh thyme or ½ teaspoon dried thyme

1½ cups French green lentils

6 cups water

1½ teaspoons kosher salt

½ teaspoon freshly ground black pepper

4 cups packed chopped chicory leaves

1 tablespoon balsamic vinegar

2 tablespoons minced scallion, light green parts only

Heat the oil in a large pot over medium heat. Working in batches to avoid crowding, add the sausage balls and brown all around, about 8 minutes, transferring them to a plate as they are ready.

When all the sausage balls are browned, stir the onion, carrot, and garlic into the fat remaining in the pot and cook until slightly softened, 3 to 5 minutes. Return the sausage balls to the pot, add the bay leaf, thyme, lentils, water, salt, and pepper and bring to a boil over high heat. Decrease the heat to maintain a brisk simmer and cook until the lentils are soft but not mushy, 20 to 25 minutes.

Stir the chicory into the pot and continue cooking until it is just wilted, about 5 minutes. Stir in the balsamic vinegar, sprinkle the chopped scallions over the top, and serve right away.

# Greek Pork and Beef Sausage with Orange Zest, Coriander, and Chile Flakes

Somewhere in the land space between Asia and Europe, pork became a rare ingredient in cooking. In most of those lands, it was because pork is proscribed for religious reasons. But then there are noticeable exceptions. In Armenia, Georgia, and Greece, pork appears on menus, though never in the exalted number of dishes that it does in the surrounding cuisines of Europe, Southeast Asia, or China. The disparity remains a mystery to me. There is no religious prohibition in these places, and pigs don't require vast ranges or grasslands to thrive. Indeed, a small pen in the home yard does nicely. Perhaps it is because of the influence of their neighbors. The Armenians, Georgians, and Greeks are Christians, but they are flanked by Muslims and, if contiguous populations don't insist on warring with one another, they intermingle, which means, most profoundly, they come together at the table. Thus, if you can't share a pork dish with your neighbors, you might instead choose lamb or beef for a multicultural, convivial affair.

In any case, the Greeks have retained in their repertoire a pork-based sausage that includes a bit of beef and is aromatic with orange zest and coriander and extra zesty with chile flakes. It imports with ease to anywhere such a sausage is wanted. **MAKES 1½ POUNDS**

1 pound ground pork

6 ounces ground beef or veal

2 ounces salt pork, fat part only, minced

1 teaspoon finely chopped orange zest

½ teaspoon ground coriander

1 teaspoon chile flakes

½ teaspoon freshly ground black pepper

⅓ cup retsina or dry white vermouth

1 teaspoon kosher salt

Place the pork, beef, salt pork, orange zest, coriander, chile flakes, pepper, retsina, and $1/2$ teaspoon of the salt in a medium bowl, and knead with your hands until thoroughly blended. Cook and taste a small sample, then add the remaining $1/2$ teaspoon salt if needed. Leave in bulk, cover, and refrigerate for at least 2 hours, or preferably overnight, to allow the flavors to blend.

Sauté or grill, or cook as directed in individual recipes. (The uncooked sausage will keep in the refrigerator for up to 3 days, or in the freezer for up to 1 week.)

# Greek Sausage in Pita Sandwiches with Cucumber-Mint Yogurt Sauce

Pita is a staple flatbread of casual Middle Eastern cuisine. Sometimes the pita has a pocket, which is opened and filled with delicious ingredients. Sometimes it has no pocket, and is merely folded over to contain the ingredients as best it can. The cooling, refreshing cucumber-laced yogurt sauce, called by many names—*tzatziki* in Greek, *jajik* in Armenian, *cacik* in Turkish, *raita* in Hindi—soothes the heat of a dish and the heat of the day. Following the Greek theme suggested by the sausage, I call for pita without a pocket. I shape the sausage into small balls and grill the balls, their aroma recalling the enticing, smoky scent that wafts from spinning souvlakis (gyros) you find in marketplaces throughout Greece. **SERVES 6**

**Sauce**

1 cup plain yogurt

1 cup peeled and coarsely chopped cucumber

1 small clove garlic, minced with ½ teaspoon salt

2 teaspoons shredded fresh mint leaves

**Pita Toppings**

2 cups cherry tomatoes, halved

2 tablespoons shredded fresh basil leaves

¼ teaspoon kosher salt

3 cups arugula leaves

1 small red bell pepper, seeded and cut into paper-thin rounds

1 cup cooked chickpeas

½ cup crumbled feta cheese

1 tablespoon extra virgin olive oil

1 pound Greek Pork and Beef Sausage (page 52), formed into twelve 1¼-inch balls

6 pita breads

To make the sauce, combine all the ingredients in a small bowl and stir to mix. Cover and refrigerate until using, or for up for 2 days.

To prepare the pita toppings, combine the tomatoes, basil, and salt in a small bowl and toss to mix. Combine the arugula, bell pepper, chickpeas, feta, and oil in a medium bowl and toss to mix.

Prepare a medium-hot grill.

Place the sausage balls on the grill rack directly over the heat and grill, turning frequently, until browned all around and no longer pink in the center, 7 to 10 minutes. Just before the sausage balls are ready, lightly char the pita breads on both sides on the grill, about 30 seconds per side. Or, toast them in a toaster oven until beginning to turn golden.

To serve, place 2 sausage balls in the center of each pita. Top with the arugula salad, then the tomatoes, dividing them evenly. Drizzle the yogurt sauce over all, fold, and enjoy.

# Pork and Water Chestnut Sausage

Water chestnuts are an underwater corm, and as you might imagine if you consider their natural environment, they are plump with water and crunchy. Their taste, on the other hand, is hard to pinpoint: it's a cross between jicama and sugarcane with a hint of nuttiness, all diluted with water. In other words, it is somewhat bland. They are often used in Chinese and Southeast Asian dishes, mainly in stir-fries, for their snappy bite. That is also what they contribute to this sausage, which features Asian tastes. I use the sausage for stuffing wontons (page 55), for making small balls to top steamed rice, for mixing into udon noodles, or for wrapping in lettuce leaves as the Thai and Laotians do with minced meats (page 119) and the Vietnamese do with savory meatballs (page 60).

Fresh water chestnuts are rarely found in markets, even those geared to an Asian clientele. They are seasonal and as much of a chore to peel as tree chestnuts (not a relative, despite the name). Canned water chestnuts fill that niche. They are available in grocery stores where even only a small amount of space is devoted to Asian ingredients. This sausage recipe calls for much less than what you get in a 6-ounce can, usually the smallest size sold. The remainder can be stored covered with fresh water in the refrigerator and used in homey stir-fries, salads, and slaws. **MAKES ½ POUND**

½ pound ground pork

2 heaping tablespoons chopped water chestnuts

1 tablespoon finely chopped scallions, white and light green parts

2 teaspoons peeled and finely chopped fresh ginger

2 teaspoons soy sauce

1 teaspoon dry sherry, such as amontillado

¼ teaspoon Asian sesame oil

¼ teaspoon kosher salt

⅛ teaspoon freshly ground black pepper

½ teaspoon sugar

Place all the ingredients in a medium bowl, and knead with your hands until thoroughly blended. Leave in bulk and shape and cook as directed in individual recipes. The sausage can be used right away, or it can be refrigerated for up to 3 days. It does not freeze well.

# Pork and Water Chestnut Sausage Wontons in Watercress and Shiitake Mushroom Soup

In the annals of folk medicine, watercress soup is said to be good for soothing a dry throat or for when a general system-cleansing tonic is needed. Here, the nip and pep of watercress infuses chicken broth made rich with slivers of shiitake mushroom and plump sausage-filled wontons to produce a new take on wonton soup that is both healthful and delicious.

Hydroponic watercress, meaning watercress grown in water and without soil, closely resembles watercress you might pick alongside a running stream in spring, but it has finer, more delicate stems and far less dirt and sand on its leaves. It is often available year-round in supermarket produce sections. **SERVES 4 TO 6**

½ pound Pork and Water Chestnut Sausage (page 54)

20 to 22 square wonton wrappers

6 cups chicken broth (page 5)

1 large shiitake mushroom (¾ ounce), stemmed and thinly sliced

1 cup packed watercress leaves and tender stems, preferably hydroponic

Kosher salt

To make the wontons, place 1 heaping teaspoon of the sausage in the center of each wonton wrapper. Lightly brush the edges of the wrapper with water, and fold it over corner to corner to make a triangle. Press the edges together with a fork to seal. As the wontons are made, transfer them to a plate. Use right away, or cover with plastic wrap and refrigerate until ready to use, within a few hours.

To make the soup, combine the broth and shiitake slices in a large saucepan and place over medium-high heat. When the broth just begins to boil, drop in as many wontons as will fit without crowding and cook until they rise to the top, 3 to 4 minutes. With a slotted spoon, transfer the wontons to a plate and repeat with the remaining wontons.

When all the wontons are cooked, stir the watercress into the simmering broth and return the wontons to the pan. Reheat gently, then ladle into individual bowls and serve right away.

# Porcupine Meatballs with Rice Quills and Hot-Sweet Mustard

These small sausage balls, with their rice "quills" poking outward, are a dream for entertaining. They can be prepared ahead of time and refrigerated for up to 2 days before cooking to serve warm. The green tea leaves season the sausage with an exotic savor, and a side plate of hot-sweet mustard, soy sauce, and Asian sesame oil for dipping, all out of a jar or bottle, suffice to complete the dish's charm. Although the meatballs have a pedigree in Chinese cuisine made with glutinous, or sweet, rice, I prefer to use regular rice.

If you don't have a bamboo steamer basket, a plate lined with lettuce leaves can substitute. The trick here is to rig up something, such as an empty can in the bottom of the pot, to elevate the plate above the water. Covering the pot will allow enough steam to collect around the plate for the balls to cook. **MAKES ABOUT 30 APPETIZER-SIZE BALLS**

**Sausage**

1 cup short-, medium-, or long-grain
  white rice

1 teaspoon loose green tea leaves, any kind

1 tablespoon boiling water

1 pound ground pork

¼ cup finely chopped scallions, mostly light
  green parts

1 tablespoon soy sauce

1 tablespoon peeled and minced fresh ginger

2 teaspoons chopped fresh cilantro

1 teaspoon freshly ground white pepper

½ teaspoon kosher salt

⅓ cup hot-sweet mustard

2 tablespoons tamari soy sauce

¼ teaspoon Asian sesame oil

To make the sausage, soak the rice in water to cover for 45 minutes. Drain in a colander, shake dry, and spread on a plate.

In a small cup, steep the tea in the boiling water for 3 minutes. When cool, combine the leaves and water with the pork, scallions, soy sauce, ginger, cilantro, white pepper, and salt in a medium bowl, and knead with your hands until thoroughly blended. Form the sausage into small balls, using about 1 tablespoon for each ball. Roll each ball in the rice, pressing the grains into the ball so they adhere. Cover and refrigerate until ready to use, up to 2 days.

*continued*

To cook the meatballs, line a bamboo steamer basket with lettuce leaves. Set the meatballs, without crowding them, on the lettuce. Select a wok that the steamer basket will fit in or a pot the same diameter as the basket so that the basket will rest firmly on the rim. Pour in water to a depth of 1 inch and bring to a boil over high heat. Set the steamer basket in the wok or on top of the pot, cover the basket or pot, and steam until the meatballs are no longer pink at the center and the rice is tender, about 25 minutes.

To serve, spread the mustard in the center of a small plate. Swirl the soy sauce on one side of the mustard and pool the sesame oil on the other. Serve the meatballs in the bamboo steamer or transfer them to a platter. Offer toothpicks for picking up the meatballs and dipping them into the mustard mixture on the plate.

# Southeast Asian Pork and Lemongrass Sausage

Lemongrass, a key ingredient in Vietnamese and Thai cooking, contributes a clean, citrusy taste and fragrance to dishes, such as in this Southeast Asian sausage, where it lightens the bold seasoning. Only the pale, tender inside of the bottom part of the lemongrass stalk is used. To prepare lemongrass cut off and discard the long, thin, gray-green leafy tops and trim away the root end. Peel away the stiff, outer leaves down to the tender core. Slice the core into very thin rounds or chop finely. **MAKES 1 POUND**

14 ounces ground pork

2 ounces salt pork, fat only, minced

2 small cloves garlic, minced or pressed

1 tablespoon finely chopped shallot

1 tablespoon finely chopped lemongrass

½ teaspoon finely chopped dried small red chile, such as cayenne or japones

1 teaspoon sugar

¼ teaspoon freshly ground black pepper

2 tablespoons Thai fish sauce

Kosher salt

Combine all the ingredients except the salt in a medium bowl, and knead with your hands until thoroughly blended. Cook and taste a small sample, then add salt to taste. Leave in bulk and shape as directed in individual recipes or stuff into sheep casing. The sausage can be used right away. (The uncooked sausage will keep in the refrigerator for up to 3 days; it does not freeze well.)

Sauté or grill, or cook as directed in individual recipes.

# Southeast Asian Pork and Lemongrass Meatball Kebabs Wrapped in Lettuce Leaves with Vietnamese Dipping Sauce

What traveler to faraway places with strange-sounding names hasn't become enamored of the street food found along the way? As much as art, architecture, magnificent landscapes, and the people, the food attracts. Street food requires no formal dress, nor a large bank account. It is simply there for eating, either at the spot or on the move to the next point of interest. In keeping with the street-food theme, grill these sausages if you can. Otherwise, a brisk sauté on the stove top works well.

The dipping sauce, *nuoc cham,* is *the* table sauce in Vietnamese dining, much like a cruet of vinegar and one of oil on an Italian table, a bottle of chile oil and one of soy sauce on a Chinese table, or fresh tomato salsa or *salsa verde* on a Mexican table. It is important to use a good-quality fish sauce, one that is smooth, rather than sharp. I recommend Thai Kitchen brand, generally available in well-stocked supermarkets these days and certainly available in Asian markets.

**SERVES 6 TO 8**

**Vietnamese Dipping Sauce**

¼ cup fresh lime juice

2 tablespoons cider vinegar

2½ tablespoons Thai fish sauce

¼ cup water

2 teaspoons sugar

5 thin rounds jalapeño or other small chile

1 tablespoon coarsely grated carrot

Peanut or canola oil, if sautéing

1 pound Southeast Asian Pork and Lemongrass Sausage (page 59), formed into 1-inch balls

24 red-leaf or butter lettuce leaves

¼ cup shredded fresh mint leaves

To make the dipping sauce, combine all the ingredients in a small bowl and stir to mix. Use right away or set aside at room temperature for up to several hours. (The sauce is best used without refrigerating and is perkiest if used the same day it is made.)

Prepare a medium-hot grill, or film the bottom of a large sauté pan with oil and place over medium-high heat. If grilling, soak 12 to 16 small bamboo skewers in water to cover while the grill heats.

If cooking on a grill, drain the skewers and thread 2 or 3 sausage balls onto each one. Place them on the grill rack directly over the heat source. If sautéing, place as many meatballs as will fit without crowding in the pan. Cook, turning the balls frequently, until brown all around and no longer pink in the center but still moist, 8 to 10 minutes, by either method.

To serve, arrange the lettuce leaves, slightly overlapping, on a platter. Transfer the meatballs to the platter as they are cooked, setting them atop the lettuce. Sprinkle the mint over the meatballs. Divide the dipping sauce among a few small bowls and set the bowls around the table so the sauce is within easy reach of all the diners. Each diner lifts a lettuce leaf, enfolding 1 or 2 of the meatballs, and dips the leaf package into the sauce.

# Beef Sausages

BEEF SAUSAGES MAKE UP a smaller menu than the extensive one for pork sausages. It seems that people prefer the large cuts when it comes to beef: roasts, steaks, or chunks stewed, braised, or skewered. But where's the beef sausage? For this chapter, I ferreted out a roundabout of traditional ways with beef sausages, and added some of my own devising in keeping with typical culinary ingredients of a certain place. I begin with meat loaf and hamburger at home, the land of vast cattle herds and more beef than almost anyone can imagine. From there I travel to cuisines where beef is available, albeit in small amounts. The sausages included are quite different, one from the other, but altogether they show the ingenious ways cooks everywhere go about making a dish with small bits of meat along with plenty of vegetables and grains, to provide a meal no one will find lacking in taste or sumptuousness.

# American Meat Loaf Somewhat Frenchified, with a California Twist

In a cross-continental sausage loaf reminiscent of French pâtés, beef, pork, and veal are combined in equal amounts with bread crumbs to make a more pillowy loaf. The California twist is replacing the traditional ketchup "icing" with pavers of sun-dried tomato across the top. You can serve it warm for dinner, American style, with a side of mashed potatoes, or French style, chilled until firm enough to slice thin for an hors d'oeuvre plate. The cooking vessel can be as ordinary as a standard aluminum loaf pan or, if you are serving it warm, a more table-worthy clay pot or round soufflé dish. **SERVES 6 TO 8**

1 pound ground beef

1 pound ground pork

1 pound ground veal

1 cup fresh bread crumbs (page 4)

1 cup finely chopped yellow or white onion

2 cloves garlic, minced

2 teaspoons chopped fresh thyme or
   1 teaspoon dried thyme

1 tablespoon kosher salt

½ teaspoon freshly ground black pepper

2 tablespoons tomato paste

⅔ cup white wine

2 large eggs

12 unseasoned oil-packed sun-dried
   tomato halves

2 ounces salt pork, unsmoked bacon,
   or pancetta, very thinly sliced

Preheat the oven to 325°F.

Place all the ingredients except the sun-dried tomatoes and salt pork in a large bowl, and knead with your hands until thoroughly blended and no longer wet.

Transfer the mixture to a 9-by-5-by-2¾-inch loaf pan or other suitable baking dish. Pat the mixture to even it across the top and fill all the way to the corners. Arrange the tomatoes over the loaf without overlapping them. Arrange the salt pork in stripes, without touching one another, over the tomatoes. Cover the pan with aluminum foil, pinching around the pan rim to seal loosely.

Bake until the juices are bubbling up clear, not pink, and the meat is no longer pink in the center, about 2 hours. Remove from the oven, uncover, and let stand at room temperature for at least 1 hour to allow the juices to settle and the loaf to firm.

Cut the meat loaf into slices as thick as you like and serve warm. Or, refrigerate overnight and serve cold.

# My House Hamburger with Pickled Red Onions, Dijon Mayonnaise, and Shredded Romaine in a Ciabatta Bun

Hamburgers reign supreme in the annals of American food, indeed in the annals of fast food around the world. Establishments that proffer them have made incursions into seemingly unlikely places to the extent that it is hardly surprising to see hamburgers on menus almost anywhere from Paris to Beijing. In fact, the humble beef patties have become such big business that there's just no stopping them.

And what is this icon of American enterprise? The answer is simple: it's ground beef seasoned with salt. In other words, hamburger is quintessential sausage, and people love it. So do I. In fact, hamburgers-for-dinner is one of my default meals. For my house hamburger, I choose organic, pasture-raised beef, which, though slightly more expensive, is definitely tastier and more healthful than average ground beef. I lightly season the meat with salt and chill it for a few hours to let the salt do its work tenderizing the meat and making it more succulent. The Dijon mayo, pickled onions, and crunchy lettuce are fundamental, as are the artisanal buns, my favorite being *ciabatta* buns. Where are the tomatoes? I left them by the wayside in the development of my house hamburger. Their acid element and red color is supplied by the pickled onions. But, sometimes I add sliced heirloom tomatoes if it's tomato season, or perhaps a splash of ketchup on one side of the bun. A hamburger is, after all, a personal thing, subject to whims of the moment. **SERVES 6**

**Hamburgers**

2½ pounds best-quality ground beef

1½ teaspoons kosher salt

**Mayonnaise**

1 large egg

2 teaspoons Dijon mustard

½ teaspoon fresh lemon juice

½ teaspoon kosher salt

½ cup extra virgin olive oil

½ cup peanut oil

**Pickled Onions**

1 large red onion, sliced into thin rounds

¼ teaspoon kosher salt

2 tablespoons red wine vinegar

2 tablespoons water

1 tablespoon sugar

Extra virgin olive oil, if cooking in a skillet

6 mini *ciabatta* or other buns, split

3 cups shredded romaine lettuce leaves

*continued*

Place the beef in a medium bowl, sprinkle with the salt, and lightly mix with your hands until thoroughly blended. Cover and refrigerate for at least 4 hours or up to overnight.

To make the mayonnaise, in a food processor, combine the egg, mustard, lemon juice, and salt and process until thoroughly blended. With the motor running, slowly drizzle in the oils to make a thick emulsion. Transfer to a small bowl, cover, and refrigerate until ready to use or for up to 5 days.

To make the pickled onions, toss together the onions and salt in a medium bowl. Combine the vinegar, water, and sugar in a small saucepan and bring to a boil, stirring to dissolve the sugar. Pour the hot mixture over the onions, stir well, and set aside for at least 1 hour or up to overnight.

To cook the burgers, prepare a medium-hot grill or film a large, heavy skillet, preferably cast iron, with oil and place over medium-high heat. Divide the ground beef into 6 equal portions, and form each portion into a patty about $1/2$ inch thick. Place the patties on the grill directly over the heat source or in the hot skillet. Cook, turning 2 or 3 times, until medium-rare, about 9 minutes, by either method, or until as done as you like.

Toast the *ciabatta*, cut sides down, on the grill or cut sides up in a toaster oven for 1 to 2 minutes until beginning to turn golden.

Sandwich a patty between bun halves and serve at once. Pass the mayonnaise, pickled onions, and lettuce on the side to be added as desired.

# Skillet Tamale Pie with Mexican Beef Sausage in Jalapeño and Cheese Corn Bread Crust

There's a certain romance associated with skillet cooking in American cuisine. It conjures campfires or rustic wood-fired ovens, where the cooking vessel must be sturdy enough to withstand the heat. Cast-iron pans fit that bill and more. I routinely use three cast-iron skillets of different sizes to accommodate different types of dishes: a small one for cooking up sausage samples for tasting or for frying up a couple of burgers; a medium size for cooking plate-size pancakes or a fat, juicy steak for two; and a large one for searing meats or fish fillets before finishing them in the oven or for making this skillet tamale pie. Cast-iron skillets offer two more advantages: they are widely available anywhere that carries kitchen equipment, from hardware stores to gourmet cookware shops, and they are modestly priced. The drawback to cast iron is that it is not serviceable for dishes that include tomatoes, wine, spinach, eggplant, or the like, because it turns the ingredient unpleasantly bitter. Romance aside, cooking the tamale pie in a cast-iron skillet offers one more advantage. It saves on pots and dishes: brown the sausage in the skillet on the stove top, spread the corn bread topping over the sausage, pop the skillet in the oven to bake, and then serve directly from the skillet.

The quick, few-ingredient sausage is also good for tacos, topping pizza, Mexican-style spaghetti and meatballs, or in place of chorizo for egg preparations. The corn bread batter can be cooked into a tender, light bread without the sausage; use an 8-inch skillet in this case.

**MAKES ONE 9-INCH PIE, SERVES 4 TO 6**

### Sausage

1 pound ground beef

¼ cup finely chopped yellow or white onion

2 tablespoons finely chopped red or green bell pepper

2 teaspoons tomato paste

2 teaspoons pure chile powder, preferably ancho or New Mexico

⅛ teaspoon ground cinnamon

1 teaspoon kosher salt

### Crust

1 cup yellow cornmeal

½ cup all-purpose flour

2 teaspoons baking powder

1 tablespoon sugar

¾ teaspoon kosher salt

1 cup milk

1 large egg

2 tablespoons butter, melted

1 tablespoon finely chopped jalapeño chile

½ cup shredded orange Cheddar cheese

Peanut or canola oil, for sautéing the sausage

*continued*

To make the sausage, place all the ingredients in a medium bowl, and knead with your hands until thoroughly blended. Set aside while you make the crust, or cover and refrigerate for up to 3 days.

To make the crust, combine the cornmeal, flour, baking powder, sugar, and salt in a medium bowl and stir with a fork to mix. In a separate bowl, whisk together the milk and egg. Add to the cornmeal mixture along with the melted butter, chile, and cheese and whisk to mix.

Preheat the oven to 375°F.

To assemble the pie, add just enough oil to a heavy 9-inch ovenproof skillet, preferably cast iron, to film the bottom and place over medium-high heat. Add the sausage and sauté, stirring to break up the clumps, until lightly browned, 3 to 4 minutes. Remove from the heat. Spread the crust batter evenly across the top.

Bake until golden around the edges and a knife inserted in the center comes out clean, about 20 minutes. Remove from the oven and let stand to cool and firm slightly before serving.

# South African Sausage with Collard Greens, Ethiopian Spiced Butter, and Cashew Rice

In this pan-African menu, disparate parts of the continent are melded in a culinary way. The sausage is inherited from the Dutch colonialists in South Africa; the cashews, which were first brought from Brazil by the Portuguese, import a taste of Nigeria on the west coast and Mozambique on the east coast; and the spiced butter, called *niter kibbeh*, wafts in gently from Ethiopia. The rice and collard greens are pan-global. **SERVES 4 TO 6**

**Spiced Butter**

½ pound unsalted butter

1 tablespoon finely chopped yellow or white onion

1 clove garlic, finely chopped

1 teaspoon peeled and finely chopped fresh ginger

½ teaspoon ground turmeric

3 cardamom seeds

1 whole clove

Small pinch of freshly grated nutmeg

Small pinch of ground cinnamon

**Sausage**

½ pound ground beef

3 ounces salt pork, minced

¼ teaspoon ground allspice

Tiny pinch of ground cloves

½ teaspoon ground coriander

Tiny pinch of freshly grated nutmeg

¼ teaspoon freshly ground black pepper

2 tablespoons water

Kosher salt

**Rice**

2 tablespoons spiced butter

½ cup salted roasted cashew nuts

½ cup golden raisins

1½ cups long-grain white rice

3 cups water

6 cups coarsely chopped collard greens, leaves only

2 tablespoons spiced butter

To make the spiced butter, place the butter in a small, heavy saucepan and melt it slowly over medium heat. Add the remaining ingredients, increase the heat slightly, and bring slowly to a boil. Decrease the heat to very low and cook, uncovered, until the milk solids on the bottom are golden and the butter fat on the top is clear, about 45 minutes. Remove from the heat and let cool to room temperature. Strain through a fine-mesh sieve lined with a double layer of cheesecloth into a small bowl. Transfer the clear liquid to a small jar and refrigerate until ready to use.

*continued*

To make the sausage, place all the ingredients except the salt in a medium bowl, and knead with your hands until thoroughly blended. Cook and taste a small sample, then add salt if needed. Form into 1-inch balls, place on a plate, cover, and set aside in the refrigerator until ready to use, or for up to overnight.

To make the rice, heat the butter in a small, heavy saucepan over medium-high heat. Add the cashews and cook, stirring, until beginning to turn golden. Add the raisins and rice and stir to coat with the butter. Add the water and bring to a boil. Decrease the heat until the water is barely shuddering. Cover the pot, set the timer for 22 minutes, and let the rice cook without lifting the lid. When the timer sounds, the water will have been absorbed and the rice will be tender. Remove from the heat and set aside to steam dry and finish cooking for 10 to 15 minutes. Fluff up the rice with a fork just before serving.

To prepare the collards, bring a large pot of salted water to boil over high heat. Add the collards and parboil until wilted and beginning to soften, about 5 minutes. Drain well and set aside.

To finish the dish, heat the 2 tablespoons spiced butter in a large sauté pan over medium-high heat. Add the meatballs and sauté until browned all around and cooked through, about 15 minutes. Add the collards to the pan and continue cooking until they are tender, 6 to 7 minutes.

Transfer to a serving dish and serve right away, with the rice on the side.

## CLEAR BUTTERS

*Niter kibbeh* is basically ghee, the preferred cooking fat of India, but seasoned with spices and a bit of onion. Both *niter kibbeh* and ghee are versions of clarified butter. They are drawn butters, meaning the milk solids have been extracted by gently melting butter to separate the fat from the solids, called the dross. The pure butter fat is poured off and the dross, left on the bottom, is discarded. The result is a sweeter, richer butter with a smoke point that is much higher than regular butter, so it doesn't burn as readily. In addition, because these drawn butters are without uncooked milk solids that can spoil, they will keep indefinitely in the refrigerator, especially *niter kibbeh* and ghee, which are further condensed by lengthy simmering to evaporate all their natural water. They are a cinch to make, as illustrated in this pan-African recipe (page 69), and I always have the unseasoned, long-keeping version, ghee, on hand for wilting a mirepoix, cooking pancakes, shallow frying, or sautéing. A note: for making clarified butters, I use unsalted butter.

# Beef Polpette with a Cheese Center

I dub my Italianate beef meatballs with a nugget of cheese in the center *polpette*, which in Italian means "round food"—as in meatball, fish ball, rice ball—because it is a fun word to say and it describes their jolly, amenable nature. They accommodate meatball needs from cocktail-size tidbits for dipping into cherry tomato chutney (page 17) to large balls bouncing in a hearty red pasta sauce (page 73). **MAKES 2 POUNDS**

⅓ cup fresh bread crumbs (page 4)

¼ cup milk

1½ pounds ground beef

1½ tablespoons finely chopped yellow or white onion

2 tablespoons finely chopped fresh flat-leaf parsley

⅛ teaspoon freshly grated nutmeg

1½ teaspoons kosher salt

Scant ½ teaspoon freshly ground black pepper

1 large egg

½ cup shredded Fontina, provolone, or other melting cheese, shredded on the large holes of a box grater

Combine the bread crumbs and milk in a medium bowl and let soak for 5 minutes. Add all the remaining ingredients except the cheese, and knead with your hands until thoroughly blended. Cover and refrigerate for at least 1 hour, or up to overnight, to firm the meat and meld the flavors.

To form the meatballs, roll them into 1- to 2-inch balls, depending on how you are going to use them. Press an indentation into the center of each ball, tuck in ½ to 1 teaspoon or so of the cheese, and then press the meat mixture over the indentation, enclosing the cheese in the center.

Sauté, grill, or braise, or cook as directed in individual recipes. (The uncooked meatballs will keep in the refrigerator for up to 2 days; they do not freeze well.)

# Italian American Spaghetti and Meatballs in Red Sauce

Whether the tomatoes are fresh or canned is a seasonal matter: in summer, choose fresh ones; in winter, use canned ones. Both make a delicious, rich sauce for braising meatballs. When using fresh tomatoes, I like to peel them and I don't bother to seed them, but that is the cook's choice, depending on time constraints and inclination. The herbs are also a matter of choice: fresh or dried basil (the most usual addition), marjoram, or tarragon all enhance the sauce with a mildly sweet herbal presence; oregano or bay add a more assertive flavor. Spaghetti is traditional for this every-day, home-style dish, but other shapes, such as bow ties, small rigatoni, or penne, will also capture and hold the sauce as the pasta is lifted from plate to mouth. For the meatballs, I like to use my *polpette*, because their cheese centers add an extra oomph to the dish. But you can also use meatballs fashioned from either sweet Italian or Tuscan sausage with good results. **SERVES 6 TO 8**

2 tablespoons extra virgin olive oil, plus more as needed

1½ pounds Beef Polpette with a Cheese Center (page 72), or Sweet Italian Sausage (page 37) or Tuscan Sausage (page 41), formed into 1½- to 2-inch balls

2 cloves garlic, finely chopped

3 pounds tomatoes, peeled or not and chopped, or 6 cups diced canned tomatoes, with juices

2 teaspoons chopped fresh basil, marjoram, tarragon, oregano, or bay, or 1 teaspoon dried of any of the herbs

1 teaspoon sugar

1 teaspoon kosher salt

½ teaspoon freshly ground black pepper

1½ pounds spaghetti or other dry pasta

¾ cup freshly grated Parmesan cheese

To make the sauce, heat the 2 tablespoons oil in a large nonreactive pot over medium-high heat. Working in batches to avoid crowding, sauté the meatballs until browned all around, about 8 minutes. Transfer to a plate. Repeat with the remaining meatballs, adding more oil to the pot if needed to prevent sticking. Set the meatballs aside.

Add the garlic to the oil remaining in the pot and sauté over medium-high heat until it is ever so lightly golden. Add the tomatoes and their juices, the herb, sugar, salt, and pepper and bring to a boil. Add the meatballs, decrease the heat to maintain a simmer, cover partially, and cook until the sauce is reduced and no longer raw tasting, about 1½ hours.

When the meatballs and sauce are almost done, cook the pasta al dente according to the package directions, drain briefly, and return it, still moist, to its cooking pot. Cover and set aside in a warm place while the sauce finishes cooking.

To serve, combine the pasta with the sauce and meatballs in a large bowl and toss gently to mix. Serve right away, with the Parmesan on the side.

# Beef and Eggplant Sausage in Eggplant Shell Casings

*Imam bayildi*, as this dish of Turkish origin is called in Bulgaria, Albania, and Greece, and its story have a special place in my cooking repertoire and in my heart. It was introduced to me by Susanna Hoffman, my longtime friend and sometimes cookbook coauthor, who is, among other things, an esteemed social anthropologist whose special field of endeavor is Greece.

The story of *imam bayildi* has many versions, but details aside, it is essentially a tale of love and household thrift. A bride new to the house of her new husband, an imam, came with a dowry of olive oil. But there was only a certain amount. And the imam loved eggplant above all other foods. In practice, because eggplant, as it cooks, is a great gulper of olive oil, and olive oil is the equivalent of kitchen gold, the dish was using up too much of the bride's dowry. What to do? How to please the husband and keep the eggplant rich and unctuous without blowing the kitchen budget?

Susanna solved the dilemma by having the thoughtful bride coax the eggplant into softening with the addition of some water, thereby requiring less of the precious olive oil and with equally excellent results. Was the imam thrilled? Did he faint as the original story line suggests? We don't know, but we presume the clever, money-minded bride kept her place and the imam was happy. In yet another, latter-day telling of the story, I call the beef and eggplant filling a sausage and the eggplant shells the casing, and *imam bayildi* winds up in a new sausage cookbook. **SERVES 4 TO 6**

**Sausage**

2 small eggplants (about ¾ pound each)

1½ teaspoons kosher salt

¼ cup extra virgin olive oil

1 yellow or white onion, finely chopped

4 cloves garlic, finely chopped

¾ pound ground beef

1½ tablespoons tomato paste

3 teaspoons chopped fresh oregano or 1 teaspoon dried oregano

1 cup red wine

2 tablespoons extra virgin olive oil, or more if needed

1 cup freshly grated Parmesan or other hard cheese

To make the sausage, cut the eggplants in half lengthwise. Scoop the pulp out of each eggplant half, leaving a $1/4$-inch-thick shell. Coarsely chop the pulp and sprinkle it with the salt. Set the pulp and shells aside separately.

In a large nonreactive sauté pan, heat the oil over medium-high heat. Add the onion and garlic and cook until wilted, about 5 minutes. Crumble in the beef and cook, stirring to break up the clumps, until the meat is browned, about 5 minutes. Stir in the tomato paste, oregano, wine, and eggplant pulp and decrease the heat to maintain a brisk simmer. Cook, stirring frequently and adding a little water when necessary to keep the mixture from sticking to the pan, until the eggplant collapses into a puree, the wine is no longer raw, and the mixture is almost dry, about 30 minutes.

Meanwhile, heat the 2 tablespoons oil in a large sauté pan over medium-high heat. Add as many eggplant shells as will fit without crowding and sauté, turning two or three times, until wilted all around, about 6 minutes. Transfer the shells, open sides up, to a baking dish in which all the shells will fit tightly packed. Repeat with the remaining shells, adding more oil if needed to prevent sticking.

Preheat the oven to 350°F. Divide the sausage mixture evenly among the eggplant shells, filling them to the top. Pour water into the baking dish to reach $1/4$ inch up the sides of the shells.

Bake until the shells are soft and the filling is bubbling up, 45 minutes to 1 hour. Sprinkle the cheese evenly over the tops of the filled shells and continue baking until the cheese is melted.

Serve hot from the oven, at room temperature, or chilled.

# Swedish Potato and Beef Sausage with Roasted Beets and Sour Cream

Partially cooking the potato and chilling it before grating serves two purposes: the potato gets thoroughly cooked within the sausage mix, which it won't if it is added raw, and the sausage doesn't turn out soft and mushy, which it will if the potato is cooked and mashed first. I prefer to get a jump start on this dish by preparing the potato a day ahead and chilling it overnight. But if you're in a rush, several hours will do the trick, in which case, use the freezer to hasten the chilling. Rather than the standard Swedish accompaniment of mashed potatoes, I serve the sausage with a side of colorful, almost candylike roasted beets topped with sour cream. **SERVES 6**

**Sausage**

1 large russet potato (10 ounces)

½ pound ground beef

2 ounces salt pork, minced

2 tablespoons finely chopped yellow or white onion

Rounded ¼ teaspoon ground allspice

Rounded ¼ teaspoon freshly ground white pepper

2 tablespoons heavy cream

Kosher salt

**Beets**

18 baby or 3 medium beets, preferably a variety of colors

1½ tablespoons extra virgin olive oil

2 tablespoons balsamic vinegar

2 tablespoons butter, or more if needed, for sautéing the sausages

1 cup sour cream

To make the sausage, peel the potato, cut it in half crosswise. Place the halves in a medium pot, add water to cover, and bring to a boil over high heat. Cook briskly until a fork can pierce through the outside but meets resistance at the center, about 8 minutes. Drain, cool, and chill in the refrigerator for at least 4 hours, or preferably overnight.

Grate the potato on the large holes of a box grater and transfer to a medium bowl. Add the beef, salt pork, onion, allspice, pepper, and cream, and knead with you hands until thoroughly blended. Cook and taste a small sample, then add salt if needed. Stuff into hog casing or form into ¼-inch-thick patties. Use right away, or cover and refrigerate for up to overnight.

*continued*

To prepare the beets, preheat the oven to 375°F. Place the unpeeled beets in a baking dish large enough to hold them in a single loose layer and add the oil and a splash of water. Cover with aluminum foil and bake until tender, about 45 minutes for baby beets and about 1 hour for medium beets. Remove from the oven and let stand until cool enough to handle. Peel the beets while they are still warm and cut into halves, quarters, or wedges about 3/4 inch wide, depending on their size. Place in a medium bowl, add the vinegar, and toss to coat. Set aside.

To cook the sausage, melt the 2 tablespoons butter in a medium sauté pan over medium-high heat. Add as many links or patties as will fit without crowding and cook, turning once or twice, until slightly golden and cooked through, 10 to 12 minutes. Transfer to a platter. If necessary, continue with another round, adding more butter to the pan as needed.

To serve, garnish the beets with a few dollops of sour cream and serve alongside the sausage. Pass the remaining sour cream in a bowl at the table.

# Savory Bread Pudding with English Sausage, Wilted Leeks, and Dried Pears

Faced with a surplus of leftover bread—enough crumbs stockpiled and nothing requiring croutons at the moment—I turn to a savory bread pudding. Since bread puddings remind me of British cooking, I whip up a sausage with typical English aromatics, add dried pear for tasty curiosity, and *ecco!*—a pudding-pie for dinner. The dried pears should be unsulfured, rather than sulfured, because they are less sweet, making them more suitable for this dish. **SERVES 4 TO 6**

**Sausage**

½ pound ground beef

1 ounce salt pork, minced

1 tablespoon fresh bread crumbs (page 4)

½ teaspoon dry mustard

⅛ teaspoon freshly grated nutmeg

½ teaspoon powdered ginger

¼ teaspoon dried sage

¼ teaspoon dried summer savory

⅛ teaspoon freshly ground black pepper

1 tablespoon water

Kosher salt

**Pudding**

2 tablespoons butter

1 cup thinly sliced leeks, white and light green parts

⅓ cup chopped dried pear halves, preferably unsulfured

¼ cup water

3 large eggs

2 cups milk

4 cups cubed day-old baguette or other artisanal country-style bread with crust (1-inch cubes)

1 teaspoon kosher salt

¾ teaspoon freshly ground black or white pepper

To make the sausage, place all the ingredients except the salt in a medium bowl, and knead with your hands until thoroughly blended. Cook and taste a small sample, then add salt if needed. Use right away, or cover and refrigerate for up to 2 days.

To make the pudding, preheat the oven to 350°F. Lightly butter a 3-quart baking dish.

In a medium sauté pan, melt the butter over medium-high heat. Add the leeks and pears and stir to mix. Add the water, decrease the heat, and cook gently until the leeks wilt but remain bright green, 3 to 5 minutes. Remove from the heat and let cool slightly.

In a large bowl, whisk together the eggs and milk. Add the bread, leek-pear mixture, salt, and pepper, and then add the sausage, breaking it into small clumps. Stir to mix and pour into the prepared dish.

Bake until toasted on the top and a knife inserted in the center comes out clean, 50 to 55 minutes. Let rest for at least 10 minutes or up to 30 minutes before serving. Serve warm.

# East European Caraway Beef and Rice Sausage

The countries of east Europe are a disparate lot, continually at odds over issues of religion and governance. But, as nearby neighbors, they share a cooking culture over and above those differences. This sausage and the following recipe for Hungarian meatballs in a sour cream sauce are my imaginative combining of the foods that this corner of the world can share without rancor or strife. The sausage, formed into balls and sautéed, can also be served with cucumbers in a light vinaigrette and potato salad dressed with dill and sour cream for a meze plate. **MAKES 1 POUND**

1 pound ground beef

1 cup steamed white rice (page 7), cooled

¼ cup minced white or yellow onion

½ teaspoon caraway seeds

1 teaspoon hot or sweet Hungarian paprika

1 teaspoon chopped fresh marjoram
   or ½ teaspoon dried marjoram

1 teaspoon kosher salt

¼ teaspoon freshly ground black pepper

Place all the ingredients in a bowl, and knead with your hands until thoroughly blended. Cover and refrigerate for at least 1 hour, or up to overnight, to firm the mixture.

Leave in bulk and shape and cook as directed in individual recipes.

# Hungarian Meatballs in Paprika Sour Cream
# with Hungarian Green Bean Salad

By curious circumstance, I found myself in Vienna in 1968, shortly after the Soviet invasion of Czechoslovakia and just over a decade after the Soviet invasion of Hungary. I was there for the International Philosophical Congress, which didn't hold my interest long. There was much more to see and experience outside the confines of academia. Aside from the eternal beauty of Vienna as a center for music, the fine arts, and fine pastries, the streets were filled with people—Czechs as well as Hungarians—who had taken refuge in the welcoming city following the invasion of their countries. The energizing buzz over the politics of the time was everywhere, expressed in Czech, Russian, Hungarian Magyar (a language unrelated to nearly all other European languages and incomprehensible to ears unfamiliar with it), and in other tongues as well. But, as always, the food served as a binding, cohesive force. The city's dining establishments, casual bistros and more formal restaurants alike, were filled with east Europeans, Viennese locals, and tourists like me, all looking for something good to eat. In addition to the impossible-to-resist Viennese fare, there were many Hungarian dishes which had become a familiar part of Viennese cooking. That is when and where I discovered the essential tastes and food combinations of east European cuisine, and, more important, that no matter what, food of the homeland is never left behind. **SERVES 4**

**Green Bean Salad**

1 pound green beans, trimmed and left whole if small or cut into 1- to 2-inch lengths if large

3 tablespoons extra virgin olive oil

1½ tablespoons cider or sherry vinegar

1 shallot, minced

¼ cup chopped fresh flat-leaf parsley

½ teaspoon dry mustard

Kosher salt and freshly ground black pepper

**Meatballs**

2 tablespoons extra virgin olive or canola oil

1 pound East European Caraway Beef and Rice Sausage (page 80), formed into 1½-inch balls

½ cup finely chopped yellow or white onion

½ cup water

2 teaspoons sweet Hungarian paprika

1 green bell pepper, quartered, seeded, and cut lengthwise into ¼-inch-wide strips

1½ cups peeled, seeded, and coarsely chopped tomatoes (fresh or canned)

1 teaspoon kosher salt

½ cup sour cream

*continued*

**Hungarian Meatballs in Paprika Sour Cream with Hungarian Green Bean Salad,** *continued*

First, make the green bean salad so it can marinate. Bring a large pot of salted water to a boil over high heat. Add the green beans and cook rapidly until quite limp and tender but still bright green, 5 to 10 minutes, depending on the size of the green beans. Drain and transfer to a serving bowl. Whisk together the oil, vinegar, shallot, parsley, and mustard. Pour the dressing over the beans and toss to mix. Season with salt and pepper and set aside at room temperature for 1 hour, or refrigerate for up to several hours, but not overnight.

To cook the meatballs, heat the oil in a large sauté pan over medium heat. Add the meatballs and sauté until lightly browned all around, 3 to 5 minutes. Transfer the meatballs to a plate, leaving the fat in the pan.

With the pan still over medium heat, add the onion and stir to coat with the fat. Add the water, paprika, bell pepper, tomatoes, and salt and stir to mix. Return the meatballs to the pan, turn them gently about to mix them in, cover the pan, and gently simmer until they are no longer pink in the center and the vegetables are tender, 15 to 20 minutes.

In a small bowl, whisk the sour cream until smooth. Add it to the sauté pan and stir gently to combine.

Spoon the meatballs and sauce into a serving dish and serve hot, with the green bean salad on the side.

# Hmong-Style Asian Greens Soup
# with Beef Meatballs and Slab Bacon

Hmong farmers, fleeing Laos to escape persecution, began arriving in the United States in the latter half of the 1970s, with the majority arriving in the 1980s. Most of them eventually settled where they could continue their agrarian life: Minnesota, Wisconsin, Ohio, North Carolina, and California, especially in the fertile land around Fresno, California. This occurrence is especially remarkable to me because it is where my Armenian relatives also settled three generations ago to farm in one of most bountiful growing places in the world. And I benefit still from that abundance.

Notwithstanding the lengthy trip to the Bay Area, Hmong-grown vegetables from Fresno appear in glorious array at my local Oakland farmers' market every Saturday, alongside the Armenian stand from the same area with its effusive display of fruits, heirloom tomatoes, eggplants, and Armenian cucumbers. Among the Hmong staples for sale are sturdy Asian brassicas, such as Chinese cabbage, Chinese mustard greens, and choys of several kinds; luffa (ridged gourd) and Chinese bitter melon; okra and small pickling cucumbers for my holiday pickle jars; and long beans for my Asian-to-new-Californian dishes. Together these two vendors supplement each other and pay tribute to the marriage of Asian and Mediterranean culinary ingredients in California's hot and prolific Central Valley. It's enough to incite a food frenzy and cook up something healthful and delicious, such as this hearty yet delicate Hmong-style main-dish soup. **SERVES 4**

**Meatballs**

1 pound ground beef

2 teaspoons minced green chiles, such as
 serrano, jalapeño, or Thai bird

¼ cup finely chopped scallions, white and
 light green parts

¼ teaspoon Asian sesame oil

¾ teaspoon freshly ground black pepper

1½ teaspoons kosher salt

**Soup**

2 teaspoons peanut or canola oil

6 ounces slab bacon, cut into 1-inch squares
 ¼ inch thick

½ cup thinly sliced leeks, white and light
 green parts, or ½ white onion, sliced
 ¼ inch thick

8 cups water

1 teaspoon kosher salt

1½ pounds Chinese mustard greens or
 Chinese cabbage, trimmed and coarsely
 chopped

Steamed white rice, for serving (page 7)

To make the meatballs, place all the ingredients in a medium bowl, and knead with your hands until thoroughly blended. Form into 12 walnut-size balls. Set aside on a plate at room temperature for up to 30 minutes, or cover and refrigerate for up to overnight.

To make the soup, heat the oil in a large pot over medium heat. Add the bacon and leeks, decrease the heat to medium-low, and cook gently until both are wilted, about 2 minutes. Add the water and salt and bring to a boil over high heat. Decrease the heat to maintain a simmer and cook, stirring occasionally, until the bacon fat is translucent, about 10 minutes. Add the meatballs and continue cooking until they rise to the top, about 5 minutes. Stir in the greens and cook until they are soft but still bright green, 3 to 5 minutes more.

Place a portion of rice in each of 4 large, wide bowls. Ladle the soup over the rice and serve right away.

# Vietnamese-Style Beef Sausage and Vegetable Spring Rolls with Mint Dipping Sauce

My love of rice paper began in childhood with candies that came packaged in colorful boxes, mostly pinkish and with children pictured gleefully jumping. Inside were gummy candies, chewable like jujubes, only softer. The fun part was unwrapping the outer paper and getting to the inside wrapping. At first it seemed like another layer of paper, a bit stiff like cellophane. But then you would pop the candy into your mouth and let the wrapping hydrate until soft enough to chew. I always found it a thrill "eating" my way from seemingly inedible paper to edible candy. So it is with rice paper wrappers for Vietnamese spring rolls" What seems at first glance a large plastic disk not for consumption, with hydration becomes supple enough to enfold all manner of comestibles. **MAKES 6 SPRING ROLLS**

### Sausage

½ pound ground beef

1 teaspoon finely chopped fresh cilantro

1 teaspoon finely chopped fresh mint

1 teaspoon finely chopped scallion

¼ teaspoon chile flakes

1 tablespoon Thai fish sauce

1 teaspoon fresh lime juice

### Dipping Sauce

¼ cup finely shredded fresh mint leaves

1 teaspoon finely chopped small green chile

1 small clove garlic, finely chopped

1 teaspoon sugar

1 tablespoon Thai fish sauce

3 tablespoons fresh lime juice

2 tablespoons water

Peanut or canola oil, for sautéing the sausage

6 dried rice paper wrappers, about
   8½ inches in diameter

6 large red- or green-leaf lettuce leaves

Handful of bean sprouts

1 carrot, peeled and coarsely grated

½ cup coarsely grated daikon

2 scallions, white and light green parts, thinly
   slivered lengthwise

To make the sausage, place all the ingredients in a medium bowl, and knead with your hands until thoroughly blended. Use right away, or cover and refrigerate for up to overnight.

To make the sauce, combine all the ingredients in a small bowl and stir to mix. Set aside.

To cook the sausage, film the bottom of a medium sauté pan with oil and place over medium-high heat. Add the sausage and sauté, stirring to break it into small clumps, until browned, 5 to 6 minutes. Remove from the heat and set aside.

To make the spring rolls, lay 1 or 2 of the rice paper wrappers on a counter and spray or brush them generously with water without saturating them. Let hydrate and soften until pliable, 1 to 2 minutes. Place a lettuce leaf in the center of each wrapper, top with about $1/4$ cup of the sausage, then with some bean sprouts, carrot, daikon, and scallion. Roll up the wrapper burrito-style, first folding the edge nearest you one-third of the way over the ingredients, then tucking in the sides, and finally folding the rest of the way to make a fat cylinder. Set on a platter and cover with plastic wrap to prevent drying out while you continue to fill the remaining rice paper wrappers. Serve right away, or leave at room temperature for up to 4 hours before serving.

To serve, remove the plastic wrap and accompany with the dipping sauce.

## WORKING WITH DRIED RICE PAPER WRAPPERS

**Dried rice paper wrappers are generally available in supermarkets and upscale grocery stores that maintain an Asian foods section. To use the wrappers, they must be hydrated. I have found that the best way to do that is to use either a spray bottle that emits a fine mist or a pastry brush. One or two at a time, moisten the wrappers with just enough water to dampen them without puddling, or they will disintegrate before your eyes. Let them sit for a minute or two until pliable enough to fold up easily without cracking (still too dry) or tearing (too wet). This usually takes one or two practice runs before you get it right. Don't despair, however. Packages contain many wrappers, so you can sacrifice a few for the sake of beauty and finesse. Once filled and rolled, the packets will keep covered with plastic wrap for a few hours. The unused wrappers will keep in the pantry virtually forever.**

# Lamb Sausages

LAMB BECKONS AN AMAZING VARIETY of ingredients to join it at table: yogurt; dried fruits; nuts; aromatic spices like nutmeg, cardamom, peppercorns, cumin, and turmeric known only to the Old World before the Age of Discovery; Old World grains like pearl barley, bulgur, and rice; and staple legumes such as chickpeas and lentils. Lamb itself was an Old World meat, but once it was carried across the Atlantic to the New World, it easily cozied up with the native vegetable offerings there: tomatoes, potatoes, bell peppers, chiles, green beans, zucchini. In other words, lamb's "natural" culinary companions quickly spanned the globe. In this chapter, an international menu of sausage recipes shows off lamb's agility in adapting to nearly whatever the pantry holds.

# Lamb and Rice Sausage for Stuffing Leaves and Vegetables

A constant—an icon—of my Armenian American childhood were grape leaves, cabbage leaves, bell peppers, zucchini, and tomatoes wrapped around or stuffed with lamb and rice sausage. My mother, a native of the American Southwest, married my father, an Armenian who enjoyed the honor of being the first of his direct family line to be born in the United States. So, in our family it was he who carried forward the Armenian tradition of lamb at table. That was not difficult for my mother to accommodate: her father was a rancher who raised sheep from time to time. In other words, lamb was a food that my parents easily shared through their more than half century of marriage.

Interestingly, though the sausage stuffing was the same whether it was tucked into grape leaves, cabbage leaves, or vegetables, there was a name distinction: wrapped in leaves, the dish was called *sarma*, but stuffed into vegetables, it was dolma. Dolmas and *sarma* made with cabbage leaves were considered family fare, and they were a dinner staple in our household. Stuffed grape leaves, which require more time and earnest effort, were festive fare, so they were saved for family get-togethers or special birthday requests (mine in particular). For how to blanch and separate the leaves for making stuffed cabbage leaves, see page 151.

**MAKES ENOUGH FOR STUFFING 14 TO16 MEDIUM-SIZE TOMATOES OR BELL PEPPERS, 60 TO 70 GRAPE LEAVES, OR 20 TO 24 CABBAGE LEAVES**

1 cup steamed long-grain white rice (page 7), cooled

1 pound ground lamb

1 yellow or white onion, very finely chopped

¼ cup tomato paste

2 teaspoons chopped fresh oregano or ½ teaspoon dried oregano

½ cup chopped fresh flat-leaf parsley

1 tablespoon fresh lemon juice

1½ teaspoons kosher salt

¾ teaspoon freshly ground black pepper

Combine all the ingredients in a medium bowl, and knead with your hands until thoroughly blended. Use right away as directed in individual recipes, or cover and refrigerate for up to 3 days.

# Bell Pepper and Tomato Dolmas with Lamb and Rice Sausage on a Bed of Potatoes

Nowadays, dolmas are standard fare throughout the eastern Mediterranean and Caucasus. But it is interesting to ponder how they became so in ancient lands that never had New World ingredients until seafarers carried them to the Old World on their return journeys. To complicate the story, they put ashore in Atlantic ports, so it was still a long trek to get to the eastern Mediterranean. Nonetheless, they did, once again demonstrating the scope and power of food as a pathway of global interconnections.

Adding a bed of potatoes as infrastructure in this dolma is a particularly Greek touch, and a good one. The potatoes soak up the juices rendered as the vegetables cook and collapse into them, making a crude sauce on the bottom of the dish. I prefer green bell peppers, but it seems these days red bells are equally, if not more, favored, so I make a mix of them, including some yellow and orange ones that add sunny color to the array. **SERVES 6 TO 8**

| | |
|---|---|
| 6 bell peppers, red, green, or yellow, or a mixture (6 to 8 ounces each) | Kosher salt and freshly ground black pepper |
| 8 tomatoes (6 ounces each) | Lamb and Rice Sausage for Stuffing Leaves and Vegetables (page 90) |
| Extra virgin olive oil | ¼ cup water |
| 2 russet potatoes (about 1¼ pounds total weight), unpeeled | 1 cup plain yogurt, whisked smooth |

Cut ½-inch-thick caps off the peppers and tomatoes and set the caps aside. Scoop out and discard the seeds from the peppers and set the peppers aside. Scoop out and discard the seeds from the tomatoes, then cut the pulp out of the center of each tomato, leaving a thick shell (some seeds clinging to the removed pulp is okay). Set the tomatoes and pulp aside separately.

Preheat the oven to 350°F. Lightly oil the bottom and sides of a baking dish large enough to hold the peppers and tomatoes in a single tightly packed layer.

Slice the potatoes into ¼-inch-thick rounds. Line the baking dish with the slices, overlapping them, and sprinkle with salt and pepper. Spread the reserved tomato pulp over the top and season with salt and pepper. Fill the peppers and tomatoes with the sausage, and set the stuffed vegetables in the dish side by side, arranging them snugly. Replace the caps on the peppers and tomatoes and pour the water into the dish around, not into, the vegetables. Cover the dish with aluminum foil.

Bake until the potatoes and peppers are fork-tender and the tomatoes are beginning to collapse, about 1 hour.

Serve hot or at room temperature, with the yogurt on the side.

# Grape Leaves Stuffed with Lamb and Rice Sausage

Without doubt, stuffed grape leaves are one of my favorite foods. I even planted two Thompson seedless grapevines, the preferred variety for Armenian stuffed grape leaves, in my small urban garden, primarily to harvest their leaves rather than their fruit. Fortunately, you don't have to be a weekend backyard gardener to have the grape leaves. Due to the influence of Greek, Turkish, Syrian, Lebanese, Georgian, and Armenian cuisines and their growing numbers in America, jarred grape leaves have become available in markets around the nation, even supermarkets. Because they are large and sturdy enough not to tear as you roll them, yet still supple, I prefer jarred leaves from California's Central Valley, home to a large population of Armenian farmers who grow tomatoes for canning, fruit for drying, and grape leaves for brining. Some cooks recommend rinsing jarred leaves, but I don't. I like the briny taste they impart.

**MAKES 60 TO 70 STUFFED LEAVES**

60 to 70 brined grape leaves, not rinsed (one 28-ounce jar, with a few left over)

Lamb and Rice Sausage for Stuffing Leaves and Vegetables (page 90)

1 lemon, very thinly sliced

¼ cup extra virgin olive oil

Working in batches according to the size of your space, lay the grape leaves, smooth side down and with the stem end facing you, on a work surface, and trim off the stems with a sharp paring knife or scissors. Place about 1 tablespoon of the stuffing in the center of each leaf. Fold each side of the bottom up over the stuffing, roll up the leaf a half turn, and then fold the sides in toward the center. Continue rolling to the top to make a tight, neat cylinder. Pack the rolled leaves in a large pot, tucking them together to make a tight layer, or two, depending on the size of the pot. It's okay to have two layers, as long as they are tightly packed.

Place a plate that will fit inside the pot over the leaves to keep them from floating up, and pour in water just to cover. Bring to a boil over high heat, cover the pot, and cook for 10 minutes. Remove from the heat and let cool, still covered, until no longer steaming, about 20 minutes. Pour off the water, pressing down on the plate to drain thoroughly and keep the leaf packets intact. Set the pot aside until the packets are completely cool. Carefully transfer the leaf packets to a platter, cover, and chill, preferably overnight, to firm and intensify the flavor.

To serve, arrange the lemon slices across the top and pour the olive oil over all. Serve chilled or at room temperature.

# Lamb and Bulgur Meatballs in Green Bean and Tomato Soup-Stew

This lamb, green bean, and tomato soup-stew, known as *fasoulia* in the home of my childhood, was the by-product of a regular event: my father dissecting a leg of lamb into its parts, from the most highly treasured, neatly cubed pieces for shish kebab to the fattier but still tender parts for grinding into sausage. A sidebar of the ritual was putting the bone and all the gristly bits into a pot, covering them with water, and gently simmering them into a broth for *fasoulia*. Even though the dish was a by-product of making shish kebab, it enjoyed a humble stature on our dinner table.

These days when I desire a taste of lamb home cooking and am not deconstructing a leg of lamb, I use a bit of purchased ground lamb for meatballs. The green beans are key here, and though I usually turn up my nose at frozen vegetables, I make an exception for *fasoulia*, so that it can be enjoyed throughout the year. I find this soup-stew doesn't need anything in the way of a side dish. A slice of bread, a spoon, and family company suffice, but Armenians would include pilaf on the side. **SERVES 4 TO 6**

**Meatballs**

¾ cup medium- or fine-grind bulgur

½ cup water

½ pound ground lamb

1 small yellow or white onion, minced

¼ teaspoon ground allspice

¼ teaspoon hot Hungarian paprika

Small pinch of ground cinnamon

1 teaspoon kosher salt

**Soup**

2 tablespoons extra virgin olive oil

1 small yellow or white onion or leek, thinly sliced

2 large cloves garlic, coarsely chopped

2 large fresh tomatoes, peeled, seeded, and coarsely chopped, or 2 cups canned whole tomatoes, coarsely chopped, with juice

1 teaspoon chopped fresh oregano or ½ teaspoon dried oregano

½ teaspoon hot Hungarian paprika

1 teaspoon kosher salt

1 tablespoon tomato paste

1 pound green beans, stemmed and left whole if small or cut into 1-inch lengths if large

3 cups water

Baguette, warmed and sliced, for serving

*continued*

To make the sausage, combine the bulgur and water in a large bowl and let soak until the bulgur is slightly softened, about 30 minutes. Add the remaining ingredients and beat with an electric mixer on high speed or process in a food processor until the mixture is smooth and pasty, about 5 minutes. Cover and refrigerate until chilled and firm, at least 1 hour or up to several hours.

To make the soup, form the sausage into ³/₄-inch balls. In a large pot, heat the oil over medium-high heat. Working in batches to avoid crowding, add the meatballs and brown all around, 3 to 4 minutes, transferring them to a plate as they are ready.

When all the meatballs are browned, stir the onion and garlic into the fat remaining in the pot and sauté briefly over medium-high until the onion is wilted. Return the meatballs to the pot, add the tomatoes, oregano, paprika, salt, tomato paste, green beans, and water, and bring to a boil over high heat. Decrease the heat to maintain a brisk simmer, cover, and cook until the tomatoes are soft and the green beans are completely tender, 30 to 40 minutes.

Remove from the heat and let rest for 10 minutes before serving with the baguette slices on the side.

# Lamb and Chickpea Meatballs with an Almond Center in Coconut Milk Curry

Although I've never been to Singapore, preparing this dish leads me there in fantasy. Heady with the fragrance and the flavors of India and Malaysia—cumin, fennel seeds, curry powder—and punctuated with coconut milk and almond, it parlays into a perfect balance of hot, sweet, salty, and sour. The touch of fresh lime juice for the sour element points toward the Southeast Asian contribution in a crossroads cuisine that translates smoothly to American kitchens.

**SERVES 4**

**Meatballs**

1 pound ground lamb

½ cup cooked chickpeas, mashed with the back of a fork

2 teaspoons ground cumin

1 teaspoon kosher salt

½ teaspoon freshly ground black pepper

20 whole blanched almonds, lightly toasted

**Curry**

2 teaspoons peanut or canola oil

½ teaspoon fennel seeds

½ yellow or white onion, minced

1 tablespoon peeled and minced fresh ginger

1 tablespoon hot or mild curry powder, or to taste

1 teaspoon ground cumin

½ teaspoon ground turmeric

¼ teaspoon cayenne pepper

1 teaspoon kosher salt

3½ cups unsweetened coconut milk (two 14-ounce cans)

1 tablespoon fresh lime juice

12 fresh cilantro sprigs, leaves and tender stems only

Steamed basmati rice (page 7), for serving

To make the meatballs, place the lamb, chickpeas, cumin, salt, and pepper in a medium bowl, and knead with your hands until thoroughly blended. Divide the mixture into 20 portions and roll each into a ball. Press an almond into the center of each ball and pat to close the opening. Set aside at room temperature for up to 1 hour, or cover and refrigerate for up to overnight.

To make the curry, heat the oil in a large sauté pan over medium-high heat. Working in batches to avoid crowding, add the meatballs and brown all around, about 5 minutes, transferring them to a plate as they are ready. Set aside.

*continued*

Add the fennel seeds to the fat remaining in the pan and sauté over medium-high heat until barely beginning to turn golden, about 1 minute. Stir in the onion and ginger and cook until wilted, about 3 minutes. Add the curry powder, cumin, turmeric, cayenne, and salt and stir to mix. Stir in the coconut milk, whisking to smooth, and bring to a boil over medium-high heat.

Add the meatballs and adjust the heat to maintain a gentle simmer. Cook until the liquid has thickened and the meatballs are cooked through, about 10 minutes. Stir in the lime juice.

Transfer to a serving dish and garnish with the cilantro sprigs. Serve with the rice in a separate bowl on the side.

# Turkish-Style Lamb Sausage with Fig and Fennel Seed Marmalade

Lamb sausage spiked with pine nuts and raisins, masterful fare from Turkey found around the Mediterranean, is exactly right for a summer grill party. The figs and fennel practically insist on being combined into a marmalade to accompany the lusty sausage. It can also be used as a compote for pork or chicken dishes or as a topping for toast or scones. If you happen to have a fig tree, or know someone who does, use its leaves to wrap the sausage. They impart an aroma and flavor of cinnamon that greatly enhances the lamb and evokes the Garden of Eden, after the Fall.

**SERVES 4**

**Marmalade**

6 plump, firm figs

½ cup sugar

⅛ teaspoon fennel seeds

1 tablespoon fresh lemon juice

**Sausage**

1½ tablespoons butter

½ cup golden raisins

2 tablespoons pine nuts

1½ pounds ground lamb

¾ teaspoon minced jalapeño chile

1 large clove garlic

1½ teaspoons finely chopped orange zest

2 tablespoons chopped fresh mint

3 tablespoons chopped fresh flat-leaf parsley

Pinch of cayenne pepper

1 teaspoon kosher salt

Extra virgin olive oil, if cooking on the stove top

Steamed rice (page 7), for serving

To make the marmalade, cut the figs into halves or quarters, depending on their size. Place them in a large microwave-safe bowl or small saucepan, add the sugar, and toss to coat. Set aside to macerate for 30 minutes or so. Add the fennel seeds and lemon juice and toss to mix. Microwave, stirring two or three times, or cook over medium heat until the juices are bubbling up and are thick enough to coat a spoon, about 15 minutes in the microwave or about 20 minutes on the stove top. Use right away, or cover and store in the refrigerator for up to 4 months.

*continued*

**Turkish-Style Lamb Sausage with Fig and Fennel Seed Marmalade,** *continued*

To make the sausage, melt the butter in a small sauté pan over medium heat. Add the raisins and pine nuts and sauté until the raisins are plumped up and the pine nuts are lightly golden, about 2 minutes. Transfer to a medium bowl and let cool. Add the remaining ingredients to the cooled raisins and nuts, and knead lightly with your hands until thoroughly blended. Form into ovals about 3 inches long, 1 1/2 inches wide, and 1/2 inch thick. Use right away, or cover and refrigerate for up to 3 days.

When ready to cook, prepare a medium-hot grill, or film a large, heavy skillet with oil and place over medium heat.

Place the sausages on the grill directly over the heat source, or in the skillet. Cook, turning twice, until medium-rare, 15 to 20 minutes total, or until as done as you like.

Serve the sausages with the marmalade and steamed rice on the side.

# Merguez

When chorizo crossed the Straits of Gibraltar from Spain to North Africa, the meat of it, pork, was swapped for lamb. The mostly Muslim North Africans don't eat pork. The feisty essence of chorizo was not lost in the translation, however: the seasonings remained pretty much the same, with regional and personal variations, as always. A touch of cinnamon here, dried whole red chiles instead of milder ground paprika, maybe some cumin, maybe not, and always garlic. On either side of the straits, it's a vivacious sausage to use in dishes that want definite sausage input. Here is the lamb version called *merguez*; for the pork version, see page 24. **MAKES 1½ POUNDS**

1½ pounds fatty ground lamb, not too finely ground

1 tablespoon minced garlic

2 teaspoons ground cumin

2 teaspoons sweet Hungarian paprika

Scant ½ teaspoon cayenne pepper

¼ teaspoon ground cinnamon

1 teaspoon ground coriander

½ teaspoon freshly ground black pepper

1½ teaspoons kosher salt

¼ cup water

Place all the ingredients in a medium bowl, and knead with your hands until thoroughly blended. Leave in bulk and shape as directed in individual recipes or stuff into sheep casing. Cover and refrigerate for at least 1 hour, or preferably overnight, to firm and blend the flavors.

Sauté or grill, or cook as directed in individual recipes. (The uncooked sausage will keep in the refrigerator for up to 5 days, or in the freezer for up to 2 weeks.)

# Merguez and Apple Tagine over Couscous with Harissa

Tagine is the signature dish, *harissa* is the signature hot condiment, and *merguez* is the signature spicy sausage of North Africa. Quince would be more usual for the fruit, but they are only fleetingly available in late fall, and the stew is quite divine throughout the year. So, I use apples, available all the time. Couscous, the signature tiny-bead pasta of North Africa that fluffs up in a hot-water soak without further cooking, is the accompaniment, the bed, in any variation. **SERVES 4**

**Harissa**

2 red jalapeño chiles or ¼ red bell pepper

2 large dried chiles, preferably ancho or New Mexico

2 dried cayenne chiles

1 clove garlic

¼ teaspoon ground coriander

¼ teaspoon caraway seeds

¼ teaspoon kosher salt

1 to 2 tablespoons extra virgin olive oil

**Tagine**

2 tablespoons butter or extra virgin olive oil

1½ pounds Merguez (page 100), formed into 1-inch balls

1 yellow or white onion, halved and thinly sliced

1 turnip, peeled and cut into ¾-inch chunks

1-inch piece fresh ginger, peeled

¾ teaspoon powdered ginger

Seeds from 1 cardamom pod

½ teaspoon ground turmeric

1-inch piece thin cinnamon stick

⅛ teaspoon cayenne pepper

½ cup chopped fresh cilantro

2 sweet-tart apples, such as Granny Smiths, pippin, or Fuji (see page 102), unpeeled, halved, cored, and cut into 1-inch chunks

½ cup water

**Couscous**

3 tablespoons butter

⅓ cup raisins

2 cups couscous

½ cup sliced almonds, lightly toasted

To make the *harissa*, roast the jalapeño chiles or red bell pepper under a preheated broiler or over a gas burner, turning as needed to color evenly, until soft and the skin is charred and blistered. Set aside until cool enough to handle, then peel and seed them.

Pull the stems off all the dried chiles and shake out some of the seeds. Break up the pods a bit, place them in a bowl, and add boiling water to cover. Set aside to soften, about 30 minutes. Lift the chiles out of the water, reserving the water, and scrape the pulp off the skins of the large chiles with a paring knife. Discard the skins. Place the pulp and the small softened chiles in a

*continued*

food processor and add the peeled fresh chiles or bell pepper, garlic, coriander, caraway seeds, and salt. Process to a thick paste. Drizzle in the oil and continue processing until as smooth as possible. Use right away, or cover and refrigerate for up to 3 weeks.

To make the tagine, heat the butter in a large pot over medium-high heat. Add the sausage balls and sauté, turning, until browned all around, about 3 minutes. Add the onion, turnip, fresh ginger, powdered ginger, cardamom seeds, turmeric, cinnamon, cayenne, and cilantro and stir to mix. Place the apples on top, add the water, cover, and simmer until the apples and turnips are soft, about 20 minutes.

While the tagine cooks, make the couscous. In a small saucepan, combine the butter and raisins and place over medium heat until the butter melts. Set aside off the heat. Bring a kettle filled with water to a boil. Spread the couscous in a wide baking dish, and pour just enough boiling water over it to moisten without floating the beads. Stir to mix and absorb the water. Pour in a little more water, stir again, and fluff with a fork. Pour in a little more water and fluff up again. Add the butter and raisins, fluff up, cover with a damp cloth, and set aside in a warm place.

To serve, spread the couscous on a large platter. Spoon the tagine across the top. Sprinkle the almonds over all and accompany with the *harissa*.

## ON COOKING APPLES

The topic of apples suitable for cooking is worth some essaying. Looking back over the shoulder of history, who could predict what Johnny Appleseed would engender? Certainly his seeds turned into a world of apples. Varieties vary in flavor, which means each provides a distinct taste and texture that define how it will be eaten. Not long ago, supermarket choices were few, with the options basically pippin, firm texture and slightly tart flavor; Golden Delicious, less firm and sweeter flavor; and Granny Smith, somewhere in between the first two. With the burgeoning of farmers' markets and growth of the eat-local, eat-fresh ethic, new varieties have appeared in great numbers. They vary according to where you live. My usual choice from among those available where I live is Fuji. The best advice for shoppers is simple: choose firm, not mealy, apples grown by farmers in your area.

# Grilled Lamb Sausage in a Pakistani-Style Sandwich with Caramelized Onions, Yogurt, Cilantro, Mint, and Toasted Cumin Seeds

The Vendy Awards began in 2004 as a benefit to raise funds for New York street food vendors who were struggling to establish their right to operate in the city. The issue in dispute was that the city wanted to tax the street vendors even though they didn't operate from brick-and-mortar venues. (The issue of who has to pay tax to whom is, of course, age-old.) Fortunately, it was finally settled, and the awards became an annual New York City celebration of street food, with an informal competition for best stand decided by popular vote. On a given day in early autumn, vendors from all around the city assemble in a park (a different one each year) and proffer their take-away delights to an ever-growing number of fans.

The flavors and aromas of Pakistani and Indian cooking aced the show three out of four times, sort of: In 2006, Sammy the Halal Man won the prize for his Pakistani chicken and rice biriyani. In 2007, the Dosa Man won for his vegan dosa. In 2008, though the Calexico burrito and taco vendor won the juried prize, the popular vote went to Biriyani Cart's Meru Sikder for his Bangladeshi lamb and rice dish. In other words, the populist Vendys confirm the wide appeal of foods from countries along the ancient spice route. Note: You can also serve the meatballs and topping and garnish elements as a *biriyani* dish, over steamed basmati rice rather than folded into a flatbread. **SERVES 6 TO 8**

**Sausage**

1 pound ground lamb

2 teaspoons finely chopped fresh cilantro

1 teaspoon finely chopped garlic, chopped with a little salt

1 teaspoon ground cumin

½ teaspoon ground coriander

4 cardamom seeds

1 teaspoon kosher salt

1 tablespoon water

3 tablespoons butter

2 yellow or white onions, very thinly sliced

1 teaspoon cumin seeds

6 Middle Eastern or South Asian flatbreads, such as pita breads, naan, or chapati

1 cup plain yogurt

12 or so tender fresh cilantro sprigs

2 tablespoons finely shredded fresh mint leaves

*continued*

To make the sausage, place all the ingredients in a medium bowl, and knead with your hands until thoroughly blended. Use right away, or cover and refrigerate for up to 2 days.

To caramelize the onions, melt the butter in a large sauté pan over medium heat. Add the onions and stir to mix. Cook slowly, stirring from time to time to prevent sticking, until partially golden brown, about 15 minutes. Increase the heat to medium-high and continue cooking, stirring often, until thoroughly browned and beginning to "fry" but still pliable, about 3 minutes. Set aside until ready to serve.

Prepare a medium-hot grill.

Place the cumin seeds in a small, dry skillet over medium-high heat or on a microwave-safe plate and toast until fragrant and beginning to pop, 2 to 3 minutes by either method. Set aside.

Form the sausage into 3/4-inch balls. Place them on the grill directly over the heat and cook, turning two or three times, until sizzling and firm, about 6 minutes total. Transfer them to a plate and keep warm. Place the flatbreads on the grill and char briefly on both sides.

To serve, place 2 or 3 sausage balls in the center of a flatbread. Top with a generous dollop of yogurt, and then some of the caramelized onion, cilantro, and mint. Sprinkle the toasted cumin seeds overall, fold, and serve.

# Northern Isles Lamb Sausage

The highland sheep of Scotland and Ireland graze in rugged terrain with sparse vegetation. Fittingly, the seasoning for a lamb sausage one might find in those northern isles is somewhat understated. A few well-chosen aromatics, along with salt and pepper, suffice to make a tasty sausage that evokes that landscape and its restrained fare. **MAKES 1 POUND**

1 pound ground lamb

2 tablespoons finely chopped fresh flat-leaf parsley

$\frac{1}{8}$ teaspoon dried rosemary

$\frac{1}{2}$ teaspoon dried thyme

$\frac{1}{4}$ teaspoon dried sage

2 tablespoons dry mustard

Small pinch of freshly grated nutmeg

1 teaspoon kosher salt

$\frac{1}{2}$ teaspoon freshly ground black pepper

$\frac{1}{4}$ cup water

Place all the ingredients in a medium bowl, and knead with your hands until thoroughly blended. Leave in bulk and shape as directed in individual recipes or stuff into sheep casing. The sausage can be used right away.

Cook as directed in individual recipes. (The uncooked sausage will keep in the refrigerator for up to 3 days; it does not freeze well.)

# Shepherd's Pie with Northern Isles
# Lamb Sausage and Potato-Horseradish Crust

Shepherd's pie is a signature dish in the pubs of England and Ireland, sometimes made with lamb, as here, and sometimes with beef, in which case it is called cottage pie. The idea is the same: a simple meat pie made with a mirepoix—onion, carrot, celery—under a top crust of mashed potatoes. There's no cheese in the mashed potatoes, but when the pie is baked, the crust is somehow enriched through the alchemy of cooking and tastes as though there were.

Shepherd's pie is usually made with leftover cooked lamb. Swapping that for quick and easy homemade lamb sausage is my revisionism, to give the humble pie a fresh and lively taste. Also, to gussy it up, I use tiny pearl onions so the onion element has a more defined presence in the pie. The horseradish is also my whim, to give the dish an acrid lilt that helps lift it above what might otherwise be humdrum fare. Fresh horseradish root is often available in produce stores and supermarkets around Passover for Jewish customers; wasabi root, though not exactly the same botanically, is similar and it is available around the New Year for Japanese customers. Like fresh ginger, horseradish root can be stored in the refrigerator almost indefinitely, as long as it is kept dry. **SERVES 4 TO 6**

**Crust**

2 pounds russet or Yukon gold potatoes, or
    a mixture

Kosher salt

½ cup milk

4 tablespoons butter, at room temperature

1½ teaspoons freshly grated horseradish or
    unseasoned prepared horseradish

½ teaspoon freshly ground white pepper

**Filling**

2 tablespoons butter

16 pearl onions, peeled

2 carrots, peeled and finely chopped

2 ribs celery, finely chopped

1 pound Northern Isles Lamb Sausage
    (page 105)

1 teaspoon chopped fresh thyme or
    ½ teaspoon dried thyme

2 tablespoons tomato paste

2 dashes of Worcestershire sauce

1 teaspoon kosher salt

½ teaspoon freshly ground white pepper

1 cup water

*continued*

To make the crust, peel the potatoes and cut them into $1^1/_2$-inch chunks. Place them in a pot, add water to cover generously and a large pinch of salt, cover, and bring to a boil over high heat. Boil briskly until the potatoes are a bit beyond fork-tender, almost collapsing, about 10 minutes. Drain in a colander and, while the potatoes are still moist, return them to the pot. Let cool briefly until no longer steaming. Add the milk, butter, and horseradish and mash with a potato masher or sturdy wire whisk until no longer chunky, almost creamy. Whisk in 1 teaspoon salt and the pepper, taste, and adjust the seasoning with more salt and pepper if desired. Set aside in a warm place.

Preheat the oven to 400°F.

To make the filling, melt the butter in a large sauté pan over medium heat. Add the pearl onions, carrots, and celery, stir to mix, and cook, stirring occasionally, until the vegetables are slightly softened, about 5 minutes. Add the lamb sausage and continue cooking, stirring to break up the clumps, until no longer pink, 3 to 4 minutes. Add the thyme, tomato paste, Worcestershire, salt, pepper, and water and stir to mix. Bring to a boil over medium heat and cook until slightly thickened, about 3 minutes.

To assemble the pie, transfer the filling to a 2-quart baking dish, preferably one that can segue from oven to table for ease of serving. Spread the mashed potatoes across the top and, with a fork or spoon, lift them into decorative peaks here and there.

Bake until the top is golden around the edges and across the peaks, 30 to 35 minutes. Serve hot, directly from the baking dish.

# Scotch Broth with Northern Isles
# Lamb Sausage, Pearl Barley, and Turnips

I adore pearl barley, yet seldom remember to cook it. But at least once a year, in late spring leaning toward summer, when the weather is still chilly, I suddenly have a notion to make Scotch broth. It is essentially a homespun celebration of root vegetables bolstered by and enriched with lamb. The usual vegetable selection includes leeks, carrots, turnips, rutabagas, kohlrabies, and parsnips. Hamburg parsley, which is grown for its root rather than its leaves and is popular in northern European cooking, is also a good addition, adding herbal appeal. Unfortunately, it is so far not widely available in U.S. markets, but a garnish of fresh parsley nicely fills the herbal niche. Lamb neck and bone-in shoulder chops, the customary cuts for Scotch broth, create a meat broth as the soup cooks.

Here, I turn the lamb into sausage and use a quick and convenient-to-make vegetable broth. That way the meat is thriftily stretched while still providing its depth of flavor to the soup. I add a tablespoon of tomato paste for color and a hint of acid: perhaps a shocking sidestep to staunch traditionalists, but I think the soup appreciates it. **SERVES 4**

2 small or 1 medium-size leek, white and light green parts, thinly sliced

1 carrot, peeled and cut into ½-inch-thick ovals

1 small turnip, peeled, halved, and cut into 1-inch-wide wedges

½ cup pearl barley

1 tablespoon tomato paste

10 cups (2½ quarts) vegetable broth (page 6)

½ pound Northern Isles Lamb Sausage (page 105), formed into ½-inch balls

1 teaspoon kosher salt

¼ cup chopped fresh flat-leaf parsley

Freshly ground black pepper, for garnish

In a large pot, combine the leek, carrot, turnip, barley, tomato paste, and broth and bring to a boil over high heat. Decrease the heat to maintain a simmer, cover partially, and cook until the barley is tender, about 45 minutes.

Add the sausage balls and salt and continue cooking until they are firm and rise to the top, about 20 minutes.

Ladle the soup into individual bowls, garnish with the parsley and black pepper, and serve piping hot.

# Poultry Sausages

POULTRY MEAT IS LEAN and thus desirable for dieting reasons, but on its own it is a difficult customer for sausage making. To be delectable, any sausage needs a fat and a moistening element: Chicken fat (schmaltz) in a chicken and matzo meatball works. So does a creamy chèvre sauce over turkey and pistachio meatballs, or broth for simmering a chicken *ballotine*. The recipes in this chapter employ those and a few other ways to keep poultry sausage succulent, either without any pork at all or without a preponderance of it.

# Chicken and Spinach Crépinettes

*Crépinettes* get their name from the veil fat that is used to wrap them. They were a classic at Pig-by-the-Tail, one of the most requested of our sausages for uncountable neighborhood and family potlucks and summer grilling parties. It's no wonder. A *crépinette* patty wrapped in its transparent caul with a whole basil leaf showing through is a thing of beauty. Caul fat is difficult to find, though that is changing with the renewed interest in charcuterie (see page 154). If you prefer to keep it simple, here is the modified recipe, caul optional. Made without caul, the *crépinettes* are equally delicious, though somewhat less mysterious without the umami the caul provides, and the lovely look is simulated by pressing a basil leaf on top of the patty just after cooking. **SERVES 6**

6 ounces bunch spinach, not baby leaves

1/2 pound ground chicken

6 ounces ground pork

Small pinch of freshly grated nutmeg

Small pinch of ground cloves

1/4 teaspoon powdered ginger

1/8 teaspoon ground coriander

1/4 teaspoon freshly ground black pepper

1/8 teaspoon freshly ground white pepper

Scant 1/2 teaspoon kosher salt

1/2 pound caul fat, soaked and rinsed (see page 154), optional

6 large fresh basil leaves

Extra virgin olive oil, if cooking on the stove top

To prepare the spinach, chop the leaves and stems all the way down to the roots and wash them in a large bowl of water. Reserve the roots for another dish. Lift out the spinach and place it, still moist, in a medium saucepan or microwave-safe bowl. Cover and cook over medium heat on the stove top or in the microwave until wilted but still bright green, about 4 minutes either way. Drain in a colander and set aside to cool completely.

To make the sausage, combine the chicken, pork, nutmeg, cloves, ginger, coriander, black and white peppers, and salt in a medium bowl. Gently squeeze any remaining water out of the spinach and add it to the bowl. Mix with your hands, without kneading, until well blended. Form the sausage into 6 patties about 3 inches in diameter. If using caul, cut it into 5-inch squares. Place a basil leaf in the center, set a patty on top, and fold up the caul to enclose it. Cover and refrigerate until thoroughly chilled, at least 2 hours or up to 2 days.

When ready to cook, prepare a medium-hot grill, or film a large, heavy skillet with oil.

Place the sausages on the grill directly over the heat source, or in the skillet over medium-high heat. Cook, turning twice, until nicely golden on both sides and no longer pink in the center but still moist, about 20 minutes total either way. If you did not use caul, press a basil leaf on each patty. Transfer to a platter and let rest for 5 minutes to allow the juices to settle before serving.

# Chicken and Matzo Meatballs in Rich Chicken Broth

Uncomplicated, straight from the heart of the cook to the mouth and belly of the diner via the stove, a bowl of matzo balls in chicken soup is a sure-bet comfort food. With chicken in the matzo balls and the homemade "twice-cooked" broth, that simple bowl of comfort food becomes a substantial meal. It is a good idea to make the broth and meatball mixture the day before, so that when you're ready to eat, there's not a long wait. Also, that way you can use the fat that congeals on top of the broth, the schmaltz, in place of butter in the matzo balls. **SERVES 4 TO 6**

**Broth**

3 pounds chicken backs and wings or other parts

½ yellow or white onion, halved

1 small carrot, cut into large chunks

1 rib celery, cut into large chunks

3 fresh flat-leaf parsley sprigs

2 fresh thyme sprigs or ½ teaspoon dried thyme

4 cups chicken broth (page 5)

4 cups water, or as needed

**Meatballs**

2 large eggs

1 tablespoon butter or schmaltz, melted

6 tablespoons matzo meal

½ pound ground chicken

1 teaspoon kosher salt

2 tablespoons finely chopped scallion, white and light green parts

2 tablespoons chopped fresh flat-leaf parsley

To make the rich broth, in a large pot, combine the chicken parts, onion, carrot, celery, parsley, thyme, broth, and water as needed to cover the chicken and bring to a boil over medium-high heat. Decrease the heat to maintain a gentle simmer, cover partially, and cook until the meat is falling off the bones and the broth is well colored, about 2 hours. Remove from the heat, let cool to room temperature, and strain through a fine-mesh sieve. Discard the contents of the sieve and refrigerate the broth until the fat congeals across the top, at least 2 hours, or preferably overnight.

To make the meatballs, crack the eggs into a medium bowl and whisk to mix. Add the butter, matzo meal, chicken, and salt and knead with your hands until thoroughly blended. Cover and refrigerate for at least 1 hour or up to overnight.

To make the soup, skim the fat off the broth. Pour the broth into a large pot and bring to a boil over medium-high heat. With moist hands, form the chicken mixture into 1¼-inch balls and drop them into the boiling broth as you go. Decrease the heat to maintain a brisk simmer, cover, and cook until the meatballs rise to the top and are tender all the way through, about 30 minutes.

To serve, ladle the broth and balls into large individual bowls and garnish each bowl with scallion and parsley. Serve piping hot.

# Chicken and Almond Meatballs in White Gazpacho

White gazpacho is a soup from the time long before there were tomatoes in Spain for making chilled red gazpacho, a familiar and beloved paean to summer. But there *were* almonds, garlic, chickens, and bread. White gazpacho is essentially a mild chicken soup made forceful, filling, and hearty with a garlic-almond mayonnaise and bread soaked in the broth. To make it more sumptuous, I add chicken and almond meatballs, echoing those same ancient ingredients. It is ultrarich. A bowlful with a side dish of sturdy-leaf salad garnished with orange slices suffices for a meal.

A tip: The recipe calls for a total of ³⁄₄ cup slivered blanched almonds, divided into ¹⁄₄ cup portions for three different steps. To facilitate the division, toast the whole amount of almonds in a microwave or toaster oven until the nuts begin to brown and have a toasty smell, 5 to 6 minutes, depending on how fresh they are. Set aside ¹⁄₄ cup of the toasted slivers for garnishing the soup. Pulverize the remaining ¹⁄₂ cup in a food processor until reduced to a paste. Divide the paste into two parts, one for the sausage, one for the soup. **SERVES 4**

**Meatballs**

¹⁄₂ pound ground chicken

¹⁄₄ cup slivered blanched almonds, toasted and pulverized

¹⁄₄ teaspoon ground coriander

¹⁄₄ teaspoon freshly ground white pepper

³⁄₄ teaspoon kosher salt

1 large egg yolk

**Gazpacho**

¹⁄₄ cup slivered blanched almonds, toasted and pulverized

4 cloves garlic, smashed and chopped with a little salt

4 large egg yolks, at room temperature

³⁄₄ cup extra virgin olive oil

3 cups chicken broth (page 5)

2 cups water

1 teaspoon kosher salt

¹⁄₂ baguette, torn into 1¹⁄₂-inch chunks

¹⁄₄ cup slivered blanched almonds, toasted

To make the meatballs, place all the ingredients in a medium bowl and knead with your hands until thoroughly blended. Cover and refrigerate for at least 30 minutes, or up to several hours, to chill and firm the mixture. Form into 1-inch balls and place on a plate. Cover and refrigerate until ready to use.

*continued*

To make the gazpacho, place the almonds, garlic, and egg yolks in a food processor and process until blended. With the machine running, slowly drizzle in the oil to make a thick emulsion. Reserve the almond-garlic-yolk mixture in the processor.

In a large saucepan, combine the broth, water, and salt and bring to a boil over high heat. Add the meatballs and simmer briskly until they rise to the top and are firm, about 10 minutes. Using a slotted spoon, transfer the meatballs to a plate and set aside in a warm place.

With the food processor running, slowly pour 2 to 3 cups of the broth into the almond-garlic-egg mixture, adding as much as you can before it spills out the top. Transfer the contents of the food processor to the saucepan with the remaining broth. Return the meatballs to the broth and heat over medium-low just until beginning to steam. Do not allow the soup to boil.

To serve, divide the bread chunks among 4 individual bowls. Ladle the soup and meatballs into the bowls, and top each bowl with the toasted almonds. Serve "piping warm."

# Chicken Breast Ballotine Stuffed with Ham Sausage

A ballotine is a boneless cut of any meat, fowl, or fish, stuffed and wrapped into a bundle and braised. It is like a miniature galantine, except that a galantine is a more elaborate preparation involving the whole beast, or like a roulade, which is a simpler preparation of a piece of meat pounded thin and wrapped around something. All are a form of sausage, and the stuffing can be almost anything edible. Here, the wrap is chicken breast and the something is ham sausage. You might think of it as a sausage with a sausage filling. Fancy though it might sound, its preparation is not difficult, and the outcome is decidedly elegant. Because this is a dish where the chicken takes a lead roll, it is important to have the best-tasting chicken available: organic and with a fatty skin still on the breast. It's the skin that makes the sausage unctuous. The cheesecloth wrap ensures that the breast remains moist throughout as it braises.

I serve the ballotine warm for a main dish with the braising liquid reduced to a sauce. I also serve it chilled as an appetizer. To serve chilled, refrigerate the ballotine overnight still wrapped in cheesecloth. The next day, remove the wrap, slice thinly, and arrange on a platter. Accompany with cornichons, Dijon mustard, and baguette slices. **SERVES 4**

**Ham Sausage**

¼ pound mild ham (not smoked), coarsely cut up

1 small shallot, coarsely cut up

½ teaspoon chopped fresh tarragon or ¼ teaspoon dried tarragon

¼ teaspoon freshly ground black pepper

½ cup heavy cream

2 large or several small Swiss chard leaves, enough to cover the chicken breast generously

1 boneless large whole chicken breast with skin

Kosher salt

2 tablespoons butter

3 cups chicken broth (page 5)

2 teaspoons Dijon mustard

To make the ham sausage, combine the ham and shallot in a food processor and process until finely cut. Add the tarragon, pepper, and cream and process to blend without pureeing. Cover and refrigerate until ready to use.

To make the ballotine, bring a medium saucepan filled with water to a boil over high heat. Drop in the chard leaves and boil just to wilt, about 30 seconds. Drain and set aside to cool while preparing the chicken breast.

*continued*

Place the chicken breast between sheets of waxed paper and pound with a mallet until no more than $1/4$ inch thick. Place the breast skin side down on a work surface and sprinkle generously with salt. Set the chard leaves across the surface of the breast. Place the ham sausage in the center and spread it over the leaves, leaving a 1-inch edge exposed along the long sides. Starting from a long side, roll up the breast to enclose the sausage and then tuck in the ends. Wrap in a length of cheesecloth long enough to leave 1 inch at either end after wrapping. Tie off the ends with kitchen string, and girdle the roll in four places with kitchen string.

To cook the ballotine, heat the butter in a deep-sided sauté pan or large pot over medium-high heat. Add the ballotine and cook, turning often, until browned all around, about 10 minutes. Add the broth and bring to a boil. Decrease the heat to maintain a brisk simmer, cover, and cook, turning three times, until firm when pressed but still a little bouncy rather than hard, about 20 minutes. Transfer to a plate and set aside to rest for 10 minutes. Strain the broth through a fine-mesh sieve into a small bowl and set aside to cool while the ballotine rests.

Skim the fat off the top of the cooled broth, place the broth in a small saucepan, and whisk in the mustard. Put the pan over medium heat and heat just until the mixture begins to boil.

To serve, remove the cheesecloth from the ballotine and slice it into $1/2$-inch-thick rounds. Arrange the slices on a platter, pour the warm sauce over them, and serve.

# Asian-Style Minced Chicken Sausage with Roasted Rice Powder and Lettuce Leaves

I first tasted this delight of Asian cooking in 1971, at The Mandarin, Cecilia Chiang's celebrated fine-dining restaurant in San Francisco's Ghirardelli Square. It was made with squab, rather than the more standard chicken. At the time, it was an anomaly, and an eye-opener to me about a rich and varied pan-Asian fare that I was just beginning to encounter. Since then, culinary relatives of that Chinese classic have become looked-for menu choices in the Thai, Lao, and Vietnamese restaurants that pepper American neighborhoods. The Southeast Asian versions, called *laab*, *laap*, *larb*, or *larp*, depending on who's doing the translating, are basically refreshing sausage salads, sometimes made with pork, suitable for an appetizer or a meal, depending on how you want to serve them. They're a cinch to make at home.

Ground chicken works fine if you are not inclined to mince the meat with a chef's knife. The advantage of the latter is that the sausage has a more defined texture. The roasted rice powder is an almost-secret treasure of Southeast Asian cuisine. It keeps its fragrance and savor for weeks, waiting in the cupboard for when you would like a dash of something different, subtle and nutty, on top of almost anything. **SERVES 4**

**Roasted Rice Powder**

¼ cup white or brown long-grain or
  short-grain rice

**Sausage**

1 pound boneless chicken breasts with skin,
  or ground chicken

2 cups chicken broth (page 5) or water

1½ tablespoons finely chopped shallot

1 tablespoon finely chopped jalapeño chile

¼ cup finely chopped fresh cilantro

2 tablespoons fresh lime juice

2 tablespoons Thai fish sauce

½ teaspoon sugar

8 romaine, butter, or red-leaf lettuce leaves

2 scallions, white and light green parts,
  slivered

2 tablespoons torn fresh basil leaves

1 tablespoon finely shredded fresh
  mint leaves

To make the roasted rice powder, place a small, heavy ungreased skillet over medium-high heat. Add the rice and dry-roast, stirring frequently, until golden brown all around, 5 to 6 minutes. Let cool slightly, transfer to a spice grinder, and coarsely grind. Set aside until ready to use, or store in an airtight container in a cool, dry cupboard for up to several weeks.

*continued*

**Asian-Style Minced Chicken Sausage with
Roasted Rice Powder and Lettuce Leaves,** *continued*

If using whole chicken breasts, mince them, including the skin. Place the minced or ground chicken in a medium saucepan, add the broth, and bring to a boil over medium-high heat. Cook until the meat is white and firm, 1 to 2 minutes. Drain into a sieve, transfer to a large bowl, and set aside to cool. If desired, reserve the cooking liquid for another purpose, though it will be cloudy.

To make the sausage, add the shallot, chile, cilantro, lime juice, fish sauce, sugar, and 2 table-spoons of the roasted rice powder to the chicken. Gently toss together with your hands, without kneading, until well mixed.

To serve, arrange the lettuce leaves on a large platter. Mound some of the sausage in the center of leach leaf. Sprinkle the remaining rice powder over the top, strew the scallions, basil, and mint over all, and serve.

# Turkey and Pistachio Meatballs
# in Creamy Chèvre Sauce

Adding panache to everyday ground turkey is a bit of a challenge. Here, pistachios, orange zest, and a creamy chèvre sauce step up to the plate and bring the balls home on the first run. Serve the sausage balls with the sauce for dipping as hors d'oeuvres with cocktails. Or, cook up spaghettini, set the sausage balls on top, and nap with the sauce.

The chèvre sauce can also be used to blanket sautéed chicken breasts, or to drizzle, cooled, over fresh pear slices for dessert, accompanied with a crisp, not-too-dry Gewürztraminer or Riesling. **SERVES 4 AS A MAIN COURSE, OR 6 TO 8 AS AN APPETIZER**

**Sausage**

1 pound ground turkey, preferably thigh meat

¼ cup finely chopped pistachios

1 teaspoon grated or minced orange zest

2 teaspoons fresh orange juice

1 teaspoon kosher or fine sea salt

1 teaspoon freshly ground green peppercorns

**Sauce**

¾ pound soft goat cheese, at room temperature

¼ cup extra virgin olive oil

⅓ cup heavy cream

2 tablespoons finely shredded fresh basil leaves

Butter or ghee and extra virgin olive oil, for sautéing

¾ pound spaghettini, cooked al dente (optional)

To make the sausage, place all the ingredients in a medium bowl, and knead with your hands until thoroughly blended. Form the mixture into meatballs the size of a cherry tomato for appetizers or 1 inch in diameter for a main course with pasta. Cover and refrigerate until ready to use, or for up to overnight.

To make the sauce, whisk together the cheese, oil, cream, and basil in a small bowl. Set aside until ready to use.

Combine 1 tablespoon butter and 1 tablespoon oil in a large sauté pan and heat over medium heat until the butter melts. Add as many meatballs as will fit without crowding and sauté on medium to medium-low heat, turning 3 or 4 times, until brown all around and no longer pink in the center, about 5 minutes for small balls, 12 minutes for large balls. Transfer the meatballs to a plate. If necessary, continue with another round, adding more butter and oil to the pan if needed.

When all the meatballs have been browned, add the cheese mixture to the pan and gently whisk over low heat until smooth and runny, about 1 minute.

If serving as hors d'oeuvres, arrange the meatballs on a platter and coat them with some of the sauce. Serve warm, with the remaining sauce on the side for dipping.

If serving with pasta, add the meatballs back to the pan with the sauce and turn to coat all around. Spread over cooked pasta and toss gently to mix.

# Braised Duck Skin Sausages with Cauliflower-Horseradish Puree

Duck was frequently on my menu when I was chef in the earliest days at what was to become the internationally acclaimed Chez Panisse Restaurant in Berkeley, California. I purchased the ducks whole, with heads and feet still on, in San Francisco's Chinatown. It was always a chore to find a place to park, but I was intent on fresh-is-best even back then, plus the people and markets provided a wonderful ethnographic adventure close to home. Searching for something to do with the many necks left from cutting up the ducks, I created this duck sausage using the necks as casing. I made a broth from the bones and other trimmed bits and braised the sausages in it. Serendipity! The lengthy braising softens the skin casing almost to butter, moistening the sausages as they cook and producing a rich sauce for dressing the sausages when they are served. For this book, I have adapted the recipe to call for whole duck legs (drumstick and thigh combinations): easier to get and equally fabulous. **SERVES 4**

5 dried morel mushrooms

¼ cup brandy

6 whole duck legs

¼ teaspoon freshly grated nutmeg

¼ teaspoon dried thyme

¾ teaspoon grated or minced tangerine or orange zest

¼ teaspoon freshly ground white pepper

3 cups chicken broth (page 5)

Duck fat or peanut or canola oil

**Puree**

1½ pounds cauliflower

⅔ cup heavy cream

1 tablespoon freshly grated horseradish or unseasoned prepared horseradish

1 teaspoon kosher salt

Combine the morels and brandy in a small bowl and set aside to rehydrate for 20 minutes, or longer is okay.

Sever the duck legs at the thigh joint. Pull off the skins from the thighs and set aside. Cut the meat off the thigh bones and drumsticks, including any skin on the drumsticks. Reserve the bones. Mince or grind the meat and drumstick skin. Squeeze the brandy out of the morels, reserving the liquid. Chop the morels and place them in a medium bowl, along with the duck meat, nutmeg, thyme, tangerine zest, pepper, and reserved brandy from soaking the morels. Mix with your hands until well blended. Cover and refrigerate for at least 1 hour, or for up to 4 hours.

Meanwhile, combine the broth and duck bones in a medium saucepan and bring to a boil over medium-high heat. Decrease the heat to maintain a simmer and cook until any scraps of meat remaining on the bones easily pull off, about 45 minutes. Remove from the heat, strain through a fine-mesh sieve into a bowl, and set the broth aside until ready to use. Discard the contents of the strainer.

Stuff the sausage into the thigh skins and secure the ends closed with toothpicks. Don't worry if the sausages look a little lopsided.

To cook the sausages, film a large, heavy skillet with a little duck fat or oil and place over medium-high heat. Add the sausages and brown lightly, turning once, about 6 minutes total. Add the broth and bring to a boil. Decrease the heat to maintain a brisk simmer, cover, and cook until the skins have begun to soften, about 1 hour. Remove the cover and continue simmering briskly, turning twice, until the liquid has reduced to a glaze, 45 minutes to 1 hour more.

While the sausages simmer, cook the puree. Bring a medium saucepan filled halfway with water to a boil over high heat. Core the cauliflower and cut it into $^1/_2$-inch florets. Add the florets and boil them until they are mashable, 10 minutes or so. Drain and let cool slightly, then transfer to a food processor. Add the cream and puree until smooth and fluffy. Spoon into a bowl, stir in the horseradish and salt.

Transfer the sausages to a platter and spoon the puree around them. Pour the pan sauce over the sausages and serve right away.

# Seafood Sausages

A FABLE: One day when Poseidon, or Neptune, depending on whether you're naming him in Greek or Latin, respectively, rose up out of the sea for a breath of fresh air, he smelled a different smell. It was meat, not something familiar in his briny realm. But it was pleasing. He ordered his courtiers to bring him some tastes of this strange thing. They did, and he was smitten. Thus was born the happy pairing of seafood and meat, and hence the many dishes that issue from that union, such as crab and sausage together on a plate, shrimp and pancetta together in a ravioli or atop a zesty rice, and clams and sausage together in a bowl. Here are those four, along with four dishes that take from the sea alone.

# A New Orleans Plate with Crab Cakes, Creole Sausage, and Cajun Rémoulade

The journey of French rémoulade sauce, a classic mustardy mayonnaise with herbs, capers, and gherkins, across the Atlantic Ocean to Acadia (now eastern Quebec), the Maritime provinces, parts of New England, and eventually on to the American South is a culinary story worth telling. In the early 1600s, the first French arrived in Acadia and took up a life of farming crops and raising livestock. A century and a half later, many descendants of those early Acadians were forced from their northern homes by the British, eventually winding up in South Carolina, Georgia, and Louisiana. Those who settled in Louisiana soon came to be called Cajuns, as did their language, a lilting patois unique to the area but universally understood in their joyous music.

And rémoulade? Unfortunately, there is no accessible literature that describes how the sauce was interpreted on Acadian tables. However, as it wended its way to Louisiana, via the American Northeast and the French Indies, it underwent a gastronomic evolution, becoming more spirited with additions of minced bell pepper and celery, tomato paste, sometimes Worcestershire sauce, horseradish, and especially Louisiana's own feisty Tabasco sauce. Here is my interpretation of that well-traveled sauce, now a Cajun rémoulade, served on a New Orleans plate with crab cakes and Creole sausage. **SERVES 6 TO 8**

### Rémoulade

¾ cup mayonnaise

1½ tablespoons Dijon mustard

1½ teaspoons finely chopped scallion, light green tops only

1 tablespoon finely chopped fresh flat-leaf parsley

½ teaspoon capers

4 cornichons, finely chopped

4 shakes Tabasco or other Louisiana hot sauce

### Crab Cakes

¾ pound fresh or frozen and thawed crabmeat, picked over for shell fragments

1 tablespoon finely chopped red bell pepper

2 teaspoons finely chopped poblano or jalapeño chile or green bell pepper

2 tablespoons finely chopped fresh flat-leaf parsley

1 teaspoon finely chopped shallot

2 teaspoons Dijon mustard

2 teaspoons fresh lemon juice

½ teaspoon kosher salt

1 large egg

1½ cups fresh bread crumbs (page 4)

1 tablespoon extra virgin olive oil, or as needed, for frying the sausage

¾ pound Creole Sausage (page 20), formed into 1¼-inch balls

4 tablespoons butter or ghee (see page 71), for frying the crab cakes

1½ cups watercress leaves and tender stems, preferably hydroponic (see page 55)

To make the rémoulade, combine the mayonnaise, mustard, scallion, parsley, capers, cornichons, and hot sauce in a small bowl and whisk to mix. Use right away, or cover and refrigerate for up to 3 days.

To make the crab cakes, place the crabmeat, red bell pepper, chile, parsley, shallot, mustard, lemon juice, salt, egg, and $1/2$ cup of the bread crumbs in a medium bowl, and mix gently with your hands until thoroughly blended. Divide the mixture into 8 equal portions, and pat each portion into a cake about 2 inches in diameter. Spread the remaining 1 cup bread crumbs on a plate. Coat each patty on both sides with the bread crumbs, pressing them to adhere. Place the patties on a plate, cover with plastic wrap, and set aside in the refrigerator to firm for at least 30 minutes or up to several hours.

To cook the sausage, heat the 1 tablespoon oil in a large sauté pan over medium-high heat. Add as many sausage balls as will fit without crowding and sauté, turning 3 or 4 times, until browned all around and just cooked through, about 8 minutes. Transfer to a plate and set aside in a warm place. If necessary, continue with another round, adding more oil to the pan if needed.

To cook the crab cakes, melt the butter in a second large sauté pan over medium-high heat. Add as many crab cakes as will fit without crowding and fry, turning once, until golden and crisp on both sides, about 8 minutes total. If necessary, continue with another round.

To serve, spread the watercress on individual plates or a platter. Set the crab cakes on top and garnish each cake with a dollop of rémoulade. Arrange the sausage balls next to the crab cakes. Pass the remaining rémoulade at the table.

# Paella with Chorizo, Shrimp, and Baby Artichokes

Paella is one of the great composed rice dishes of the world. Many regions in Spain boast of serving the "finest" rendition, but Valencia, its original home, claims the blue ribbon. Many tourist guides acquiesce. Located close by the sea, the city provides its cooks with a daily supply of fresh seafood. Squid, which blackens the rice with its ink, and mussels are abundant and have become key elements in *paella valenciana*, along with snails and green beans. That repertoire has been expanded to include a selection of chicken or rabbit pieces; small sausages; other shellfish, such as shrimp, crayfish, or cockles; and other vegetables, such as red bell pepper or artichoke, though not all at once. I like to use shrimp in the shell, but if you don't think your guests will want to peel their own shrimp, you can cook them as directed, then peel them before returning them to the pan.

Paella is traditionally cooked over a charcoal fire in a large, wide, two-handled shallow pan called a *paellera*. As is common in many Mediterranean and Middle Eastern cultures in which dishes, such as shish kebab and gyros, are cooked over an open fire, the paella cooks are traditionally men because the men own fire. Nowadays, the *paellera* is more often used indoors, and women as well as men cook the dish. It is always a festive offering, worthy of a get-together of any size, indoors or out. No matter who is cooking, the key to a successful paella is the rice. It must be Spanish or Italian short grain. **SERVES 6**

| | |
|---|---|
| 24 baby artichokes (about 2 pounds) | 3 cups Spanish or Italian short-grain white rice |
| 3 tablespoons extra virgin olive oil, plus more as needed | 6 cups water, plus more as needed |
| 2 cloves garlic, finely chopped | 2 teaspoons kosher salt |
| 1 pound large shrimp, preferably in the shell | Large pinch of saffron threads |
| 1 pound Chorizo (page 24) | |

Trim off the stems from the artichokes flush with the bottom, and then pull away their outer leaves down to the inner yellow ones. Cut off the top of each artichoke down to the yellow part. Cut each artichoke in half lengthwise.

In a large sauté pan, heat the 3 tablespoons oil over medium heat. Add the artichokes and garlic and sauté, turning the artichokes often, until they are almost tender but still a little crunchy, about 5 minutes. Transfer to a plate and set aside in a warm place.

Add the shrimp, increase the heat to medium-high, and sauté until just turning pink and curling up, about 5 minutes. (Add more oil if necessary to keep them from burning.) Transfer to the plate with the artichokes.

Add the sausage and sauté, stirring from time to time to break it into large clumps, until firm, about 5 minutes. Add the rice, stir to mix, and sauté until it is opaque, 2 to 3 minutes.

Stir in the 6 cups water and the salt and bring to a boil. Decrease the heat to maintain a brisk simmer and cook, stirring often, until the rice is al dente and the liquid is mostly absorbed, about 20 minutes. (Add more water if the dish starts to dry out before the rice is cooked.)

Stir in the saffron, then the artichokes and shrimp. Cover the pan loosely with a kitchen cloth and let stand for 10 minutes for the rice to steam dry. Serve hot.

# Chorizo and Clams, Portuguese Style

Portugal lies on the Iberian Peninsula between the Atlantic Ocean and Spain, and many of its culinary inspirations pull from both those places. In the province of Alentejo in southern Portugal, a combination of pork and clams expresses the inherent poetry of this duality. Ruddy with paprika, fragrant with garlic, and redolent of salt air, it is an exotic, compelling dish in which land meets sea in a bowl. The Portuguese are so fond of it that it is exported with them anywhere they settle, including New Bedford, Massachusetts, where it is served with corn on the cob. The dish is traditionally made with pork meat, cubed, spiced, and marinated overnight. I have simplified the recipe by using chorizo for the pork. It provides the same spiciness and color while eliminating a lengthy step. **SERVES 4**

2 tablespoons extra virgin olive oil

1 yellow or white onion, quartered and thinly sliced

2 cloves garlic, chopped

6 ounces Chorizo (page 24)

1 tablespoon tomato paste

1 small bay leaf, crumbled

¼ cup white wine

½ cup water

2 pounds clams, mussels, or a mixture, scrubbed and mussels debearded if needed

In a large pot or sauté pan, heat the oil over medium heat. Add the onion and garlic and cook until the onion begins to wilt, about 3 minutes. Crumble the chorizo into the pan and cook, stirring occasionally, until it begins to firm, about 2 minutes. Stir in the tomato paste, bay leaf, wine, and water and bring to a boil. Cover partially and cook until the liquid is reduced and the mixture is saucy, 5 minutes.

Add the shellfish to the pan, cover all the way, and cook until the shells open and their meat is slightly firm, about 5 minutes. Discard any shellfish that fail to open, then serve right away.

# Northeast Coast Seafood Chowder with Codfish Balls and Shrimp in Tomato-Cream Broth

Cod, as food historian Mark Kurlansky convincingly purports in his fascinating exegesis on its commercial history, is "the fish that changed the world." Evidence exists that commerce in cod was founded in the tenth century by seafaring Vikings who, seeking new fishing grounds when their homeland supply was depleted for the season, came upon Newfoundland and its cod bounty, establishing a trade route between the Old World and what was called the New World. In time, cod commerce gave rise to emigration and engendered settlements, eventually towns, along the northern Atlantic seaboard. Naturally, the first settlers in that harsh environment created food based on what was available: cod. Although much of it was preserved with salt to use at home and to ship across the Atlantic to the waiting market there, some was used fresh, especially in chowder. In this version, the cod is fashioned into a sausagelike mixture and formed into balls, which are joined in the soup pot by another popular local catch, shrimp. Northeast fishermen harvest the pink, intensely flavored Northern shrimp, also known as Maine shrimp, which are available only from winter through early spring. But almost any medium shrimp can substitute, as long as they are from North American waters. **SERVES 4 TO 6**

## Cod Balls

¾ pound skinless cod fillets

½ cup fine fresh bread crumbs (page 4)

½ teaspoon chopped fresh thyme
   or ¼ teaspoon dried thyme

2 teaspoons grated or minced lemon zest

2 teaspoons fresh lemon juice

3 tablespoons heavy cream

1 teaspoon kosher salt

Small pinch of cayenne pepper

## Chowder

2 tablespoons butter

⅔ cup sliced celery (¼-inch-thick slices)

1 cup finely chopped yellow or white onion

½ teaspoon chopped fresh thyme or
   ¼ teaspoon dried thyme

2 cups peeled and diced russet potatoes
   (½-inch dice)

7 cups milk

1 teaspoon kosher salt

½ teaspoon freshly ground white pepper

½ pound medium shrimp, shelled

2 tablespoons tomato paste

¾ cup heavy cream

*continued*

To make the fish balls, place all the ingredients in a food processor and process to as fine a puree as possible. With moist hands, pat it into $1^1/_2$-inch balls. Place on a plate, cover with plastic wrap, and refrigerate until ready to use.

To make the chowder, melt the butter in a large soup pot over medium heat. Add the celery, onion, and thyme and cook, without browning, until the vegetables are wilted, about 5 minutes. Add the potatoes, milk, salt, and pepper, increase the heat to medium-high, and cook until the milk is bubbling up and a skin has formed across the top, about 10 minutes. Add the fish balls and simmer briskly until they are just firm, about 5 minutes. Add the shrimp and cook until they are barely pink, about 3 minutes.

Stir in the tomato paste and cream and heat through. Ladle into bowls and serve piping hot.

# Salmon Croquettes with Fennel, Red Bell Pepper, and Arugula Slaw

Before the era of widespread refrigeration, most of the commercial salmon catch was smoked or canned so it could be stored until the next season. And there was plenty to can in those days, because the salmon population was not threatened by overfishing or pollution of their habitat. As a result, canned salmon became a fixture on grocery store shelves and in home pantries across the United States, and the salmon croquette became a specialty of American cooking. I recall my mother opening a can of salmon for a quick dinner, mixing it with egg, bread crumbs, and some seasonings, patting the mixture into cakes, and sautéing them until golden on both sides.

These days, it is not difficult to procure fresh salmon, and that is what I prefer for my croquettes, though always shopping with sustainability of the fish in mind. The price difference between canned and fresh is unexpectedly small, and it takes but a few minutes to cook salmon steaks or fillets—in the oven or in the microwave—for the croquettes. The payoff is, as is generally true, the taste difference: fresh is the best.

The croquettes make a pretty focus for a brunch or light dinner menu, as here, or serve them as an unusual side dish for breakfast with eggs cooked any style. **SERVES 4 TO 6**

### Croquettes

1 pound skinless salmon fillets

Kosher salt

1 tablespoon chopped fresh flat-leaf parsley

¾ teaspoon chopped fresh tarragon or ¼ teaspoon dried tarragon

¾ cup fine fresh bread crumbs (page 4)

2 large eggs

1 teaspoon Worcestershire sauce

¾ teaspoon kosher salt

Pinch of cayenne pepper

### Slaw

1 fennel bulb, halved lengthwise, cored, and cut crosswise into thin slices

1 red bell pepper, halved lengthwise, seeded, and thinly sliced

⅓ cup fresh lemon juice

½ teaspoon kosher salt

6 cups arugula leaves

2 tablespoons extra virgin olive oil

1 cup fresh bread crumbs, to coat the croquettes

4 tablespoons butter or ghee (see page 71), or more if needed, for frying

4 lemon wedges

*continued*

The salmon can be cooked in the oven or in the microwave. If cooking in the oven, preheat it to 375°F.

To cook the salmon, sprinkle the fillets with salt and place them on a lightly oiled baking sheet or microwave-safe dish. Cook in the oven uncovered or in the microwave covered until just beyond medium-rare and white curds have formed across the top, about 8 minutes in the oven or 4 to 5 minutes in the microwave, depending on the thickness of the pieces. Transfer to a large bowl and when completely cool, pick out any errant bones.

To make the croquettes, add the parsley, tarragon, bread crumbs, eggs, Worcestershire sauce, salt, and pepper to the bowl with the salmon and mix with your hands, breaking up the salmon without mashing it, until well blended. Spread the bread crumbs for coating on a large plate. Form the salmon mixture into patties 1/2 inch thick in whatever diameter you would like, depending on how many people you are serving. Coat them on both sides with the crumbs. Set the coated patties aside in the refrigerator to firm for 30 minutes or so.

To make the slaw, combine the fennel, bell pepper, lemon juice, and salt in a large bowl and toss gently to mix. Place the arugula on top and set aside without tossing.

To cook the croquettes, melt the butter in a large sauté pan over medium-high heat. Add as many salmon patties as will fit without crowding and fry, turning once, until golden on both sides, 4 to 5 minutes total. If necessary, continue with another round, adding more butter to the pan if needed.

To serve, gently mix the arugula into the slaw. Spread the slaw across a large serving platter and drizzle with the oil. Set the patties on top, garnish with the lemon wedges, and serve right away.

# Gefilte Fish with Beet Horseradish

The Yiddish word *gefilte* means "filled" or "stuffed," and originally gefilte fish was fish skins stuffed with a white fish mousse, similar to a French quenelle. Eventually the fish skins were eliminated and just the stuffing was kept, more user-friendly for the home cook, and the skins, if there were any, became part of the broth. Once freed from being stuffed into something, the filling was shaped into oval dumplings and poached without benefit of wrapping. What is important for authenticity, and for the best flavor, is to brew your own fish broth with white fish bones (not salmon or shrimp), which is ready in only 30 minutes. Why take the trouble at all? Well, some dishes are revered for their status as iconic ritual that affirms and carries forth the culture, and making them from scratch both reinforces that role and binds the community of which they are part. Out-of-the-jar gefilte fish just isn't the same. It is a must-have dish on the Seder table, and beyond that, it is delicious for any occasion that calls for a light first course. Gefilte fish is traditionally made with freshwater fish, but if none is available, any saltwater fish with firm, white flesh will do.

Horseradish root is part of the Seder plate of symbolic foods that signify various stages of the Jews' flight from Egypt. Finely grated, and sometimes colored a fiery red with the addition of shredded beets, the horseradish condiment is both the customary and perfect accompaniment to gefilte fish. **SERVES 4 TO 6**

### White Fish Dumplings

¾ pound skinless white-fleshed fish fillets, such as trout, yellow pike, halibut, or cod

⅓ cup grated or minced yellow or white onion

1 large egg

2 tablespoons matzo meal

½ teaspoon kosher salt

¼ teaspoon freshly ground white pepper

### Beet Horseradish

1 large red beet (about ½ pound)

1 to 2 tablespoons grated fresh horseradish

1½ teaspoons distilled white vinegar

¼ teaspoon sugar

¼ teaspoon kosher salt

### Broth

1½ pounds white fish bones and heads

1 small carrot, coarsely cut up

½ rib celery, coarsely cut up

1 large shallot, coarsely cut up

1 teaspoon kosher salt

5 cups water

To make the dumplings, cut the fish into 1½-inch chunks and place in the freezer for 10 to 15 minutes to freeze partially. Transfer to a food processor and process to as fine a puree as possible. Add the onion, egg, matzo meal, salt, and pepper and continue processing to a paste. Cover and set aside in the refrigerator until quite firm, at least 1 hour or up to overnight.

To make the beet horseradish, cook the beet in water to cover until it can barely be pierced, 20 to 30 minutes, depending on the size. Drain and let cool until it can be handled, then peel it while still warm. Grate on the medium-fine holes of a box grater. In a small bowl, combine the grated beet, horseradish, vinegar, sugar, and salt and stir to mix. Set aside at room temperature until ready to use or refrigerate for up to 2 days.

To make the broth, combine the fish bones and heads, carrot, celery, shallot, salt, and water in a medium saucepan, adding more water if needed to cover the ingredients. Bring to a boil over high heat and skim off any foam that forms on the surface. Decrease the heat to maintain a brisk simmer, cover partially, and cook until slightly reduced, about 30 minutes. Strain through a fine-mesh sieve into a large pot and bring to a simmer over medium-high heat.

To cook the dumplings, with wet hands, form the fish mixture into ovals the size of a very large egg, using about ⅓ cup for each dumpling. Drop them into the broth and bring just to a boil. Cover the pot and simmer, adding more water if necessary to keep the dumplings afloat, until cooked through, about 1½ hours. Transfer the dumplings and broth to a serving bowl, let cool until no longer steaming, and refrigerate until the broth sets into a loose gelée, 3 hours or so.

Serve the gefilte fish and gelée cold with the beet horseradish on the side.

# Shrimp and Pancetta Sausage Ravioli
# with Broccoli Rabe and Edamame or Fava Beans

Delicate and unusual, shrimp and pancetta combined into a sausage is an example of the delight-ful ways in which seafood and pork can glamorize each other, here in ravioli made easy to execute using store-bought wonton wrappers for the pasta. Edamame (fresh soybeans) and fava beans (broad beans), both Old World beans, can be used interchangeably in this recipe. Both are almost meaty and bright green, and provide similar vivid leguminous presence in dishes that employ them. However, practically speaking, edamame have the advantage because they are available already shelled in supermarket freezer sections in all seasons. Favas, in contrast, are mainly spring to early summer and fall fare, and they are a chore to prepare, requiring first shell-ing and then peeling each bean after immersing in boiling water for 1 or 2 minutes to loosen the bitter-tasting skins. (A side note: if you are using fava beans and purchasing them at a farmers' market, you can probably also pick up some fava leaves. As our vegetable horizons expand more and more, they have become available and are quite tasty as a green for a soup such as this one or tossed into a salad.)

Shrimp and pancetta sausage can also be made into small balls and dropped into a chicken or vegetable broth for a substantial appetizer or light first course. Or, you can use it to top small cooked and halved artichokes, then generously sprinkle the sausage with bread crumbs and briefly cook the sausage and brown the crumbs in a hot oven or under a broiler. **SERVES 4 TO 6**

**Sausage**

½ pound medium shrimp, shelled

2 ounces pancetta

1 tablespoon finely chopped scallion, light
    green parts only

½ teaspoon grated or minced lemon zest

⅛ teaspoon kosher salt

**Ravioli**

24 square wonton wrappers

Kosher salt

2 ounces broccoli rabe or broccolini, sliced
    lengthwise into thin strips

½ cup shelled edamame or shelled and
    peeled fava beans

2 teaspoons grated or minced lemon zest

¼ cup best-quality extra virgin olive oil

To make the sausage, place the shrimp and pancetta in a food processor and pulse to chop. Add the scallion, lemon zest, and salt and pulse briefly until blended but not pureed. Use right away, or cover and refrigerate for up to overnight.

To make the ravioli, place 1 teaspoon of the sausage in the center of each wonton wrapper. Lightly brush the edges of the wrapper with water, and fold it over corner to corner to make a triangle. Press the edges together with a fork to seal. As the ravioli are made, transfer them to a plate. Cover with a damp cloth and set aside.

Bring a medium saucepan filled with $1^1/_2$ inches of water to a boil over high heat. Add a pinch of salt and then the broccoli rabe and edamame. When the water returns to a boil, cook until the broccoli is barely wilted and still bright green, about 3 minutes. Lift out the vegetables with a slotted spoon and rinse under cold running water. Set aside.

To cook the ravioli use the same pan of water and return it to a boil. Add as many ravioli as will fit without crowding and boil gently until they float to the top and plump up, about 3 minutes. Lift them out with a slotted spoon, shake to dry slightly, and transfer, still moist, to a platter. Set aside in a warm place and continue with another batch until all are cooked.

Arrange the broccoli and edamame over and around the ravioli. Sprinkle the zest over the top and drizzle the olive oil over all. Serve right away.

# Japanese-Style White Fish Balls in Shiitake-Ginger Broth

Subtle, calming, and healthful, this clear soup is a home remedy for alleviating stress. The ginger subdues nausea, aids digestion, and stimulates circulation; the fish balls provide protein to relieve hunger; and the mushrooms and spinach enliven the broth to make the remedy more than palatable, indeed desirable. How simple. How soothing.

The spinach roots add an elusive textural dimension to the broth. Not exactly crunchable, they are nonetheless more chewable than spinach leaves. They are available at the bottom of ordinary bunch spinach sold with roots attached. Cut them off to use in the soup and save the leaves for another dish. **SERVES 4 TO 6**

### Fish Balls

½ pound skinless fatty white-fleshed fish fillets, such as black sea bass, white sea bass, or butterfish

1 teaspoon peeled and grated fresh ginger

1 teaspoon fresh lemon juice

½ teaspoon kosher salt

¼ teaspoon freshly ground white pepper

### Soup

6 cups water

2 ounces shiitake mushrooms, stems cut off and chopped and caps thinly sliced

2 tablespoons peeled and coarsely chopped fresh ginger

4 cilantro sprigs

2 tablespoons tamari soy sauce

8 spinach roots, cut in half lengthwise

2 small scallions, white and light green parts, cut lengthwise into thin strands

To make the fish balls, cut the fish into 1- to 2-inch chunks, place in a food processor, and process until finely ground. Add the ginger, lemon juice, salt, and pepper and process until thoroughly blended. With wet hands, pat the mixture into ³/₄-inch balls. Set aside on a plate, cover, and refrigerate until ready to cook.

To make the soup, combine the water, mushroom stems, ginger, cilantro, and soy sauce in a medium saucepan and bring to a boil over high heat. Decrease the heat to maintain a gentle simmer, cover partially, and cook until the mushroom and ginger pieces are soft, about 10 minutes. Strain through a fine-mesh sieve into a clean medium saucepan. Discard the contents of the strainer.

Bring the strained broth just to a boil over medium-high heat. Add the shiitake caps, spinach roots, and fish balls and cook until the balls rise to the top, about 3 minutes. Ladle the soup into individual bowls, garnish each bowl with a few scallion strands, and serve piping hot.

# A Trio of
# Vegetarian "Sausages"

VEG BURGERS, VEG BALLS, VEG ROLLS—what qualifies them as "sausage"? Well, the word *sausage* comes from the Latin *salsus*, which means "salted." Sausage also means small bits, often wrapped somehow. So, why not small bits of vegetables and grains seasoned and wrapped or formed into patties? Of course, it's totally poetic license that accommodates such sidestepping. Here are three recipes in that vein: one for quinoa, one for bulgur, and one for brown rice. They all use an ancient grain as the "meat" of the matter, and they all have the special perk of enticing your vegetarian friends to table.

# Quinoa and Tofu Veg Burgers with Red Bell Pepper Sauce

Quinoa (keen-wah), though not a cereal grain because it is not a grass plant, is nonetheless a life-sustaining grain native to the Andes Mountains in what is now Peru, Chile, and Bolivia. Although it was a staple food of the Inca, who peopled those high places, somewhere along the way it got shuffled aside for wheat and rice, grain imports from the Old World, and for corn, the New World's other great grain. There it remained, in the shadows of time, until recently, when health aficionados rediscovered its food value and deliciousness.

Quinoa's nutrition is unique among the grains of the world. Within each tiny, almost miniscule bit of it, there is complete protein. When cooked, the grains puff up four times their size into a pillowy mass that resembles the cells in a beehive, with each compartment distinct. That means quinoa serves up not only plenty of nutrition but also enough bulk to make a filling meal. Together with tofu, their nutrition pedigree becomes double blue ribbon. **SERVES 6**

**Burgers**

½ cup quinoa

1 cup water

1 cup finely shredded Swiss chard

3 large shiitake mushrooms, stems removed and caps finely chopped (⅔ cup)

1 tablespoon minced shallot

1 tablespoon finely chopped fresh chives

1 teaspoon peeled and minced fresh ginger

1 teaspoon grated or minced lemon zest

7 ounces firm tofu, mashed with a fork

1 cup fresh bread crumbs (page 4)

2 large eggs, lightly beaten

1 teaspoon kosher or fine sea salt

Freshly ground black pepper

**Sauce**

2 red bell peppers, roasted, peeled, and seeded

2 teaspoons extra virgin olive oil

1 teaspoon fresh lemon juice

3 tablespoons butter or extra virgin olive oil

To make the burgers, first rinse and drain the quinoa and place it in a medium saucepan with the water. Bring to a boil over high heat, cover, decrease the heat to maintain a simmer, and cook until the water is absorbed, about 10 minutes. Set aside, covered, to cool.

To prepare the chard, bring a small saucepan filled with water to a boil over high heat. Add the chard and blanch for 1 minute. Drain well and set aside to cool.

Place the cooled quinoa, chard, mushrooms, shallot, chives, ginger, lemon zest, tofu, bread crumbs, eggs, salt, and a few grinds of pepper in a medium bowl, and knead with your hands until the mixture firmly coheres. Divide the mixture into 6 equal portions and form each portion into a burger 3/4 inch thick and 3 inches in diameter. Place the patties on a plate, cover with plastic wrap, and set aside in the refrigerator to chill and firm for 15 to 30 minutes.

To make the sauce, combine all the ingredients in a food processor and process until smooth. Use right away, or set aside at room temperature for up to several hours.

To cook the burgers, melt the butter in a large skillet over medium-high heat until foaming. Add as many burgers as will fit without crowding and fry, turning once, until golden on both sides, about 15 minutes altogether. If necessary, continue with another round.

To serve, top each burger with a dollop of the sauce. Serve the remaining sauce on the side.

# Bulgur Veg Balls in Mustard-Yogurt Broth with Mint Butter

You might not think so, but butter is as important to the cooking of much of India, Africa, the Middle East, and all the way north to the Caucasus as it is to French, Swiss, or Scandinavian cooking. So it's not too surprising to see it surface as a main ingredient in the broth for this traditional Armenian vegetarian bulgur dish. The red bell pepper and paprika tint the bulgur balls a Titian red, while the mustard and butter add a soft yellow hue to the broth.

If there are any leftover balls and broth, chill them together thoroughly, until the broth is thickened to a cheeselike consistency. Then press them together and form the mixture into balls. Drizzle with fruity extra virgin olive and serve with crackers or bread. **SERVES 4 TO 6**

**Bulgur Balls**

½ cup medium-grind bulgur

1 tablespoon finely chopped scallion, light green parts only

¼ cup finely chopped red bell pepper

2 tablespoons finely chopped fresh flat-leaf parsley

½ teaspoon sweet Hungarian paprika

⅛ teaspoon cayenne pepper

½ teaspoon kosher salt

**Broth**

1½ cups plain yogurt

¾ cup water

1 large egg

2 teaspoons Dijon mustard

2 tablespoons butter

¼ cup finely shredded fresh mint leaves

2 tablespoons butter

To make the balls, rinse the bulgur, place it in a medium bowl, and add water just to cover. Set aside to soak for 45 minutes. Drain and return to the bowl. Add the scallion, bell pepper, parsley, paprika, cayenne, and salt and stir to mix. Transfer the mixture to a food processor and process, scraping down the sides of the bowl from time to time, until pasty and slightly moist but no longer wet, about 5 minutes. Cover and refrigerate to firm for about 1 hour.

To form the balls, with wet hands, roll the bulgur mixture into 3/4-inch balls. Use right away, or cover and set aside in the refrigerator until ready to cook, up to an hour or so. Do not leave them overnight or they will become dry and crumbly.

To prepare the broth, whisk together the yogurt and water in a small bowl. Whisk together the egg and mustard in a separate small bowl. Set both bowls aside at room temperature. In a small saucepan, melt the butter over medium-low heat. Stir in the mint, remove from the heat, and set aside.

To sauté the balls, melt the butter in a large nonreactive sauté pan over medium heat. Add the balls and cook, gently turning with a wooden spoon, until browned all around, about 12 minutes. Transfer the balls to a plate and set aside.

To finish the dish, return the sauté pan to medium heat and whisk in the yogurt mixture. Cook, stirring, until it is almost at the boiling point. Then slowly whisk 1/2 cup of the yogurt mixture into the mustard-egg mixture. Return the combined mixtures to the pan, whisking gently and constantly. Decrease the heat to medium-low and bring almost to a boil, taking care not to let the mixture actually boil. Add the butter-mint mixture and swirl it around without mixing it in.

To serve, return the balls to the pan and heat, still taking care not to let the broth boil. Ladle the bulgur balls and broth into individual wide bowls and serve steaming hot.

# Brown Rice, Walnut, and Dandelion Green Veg Sausage Wrapped in Cabbage Leaves with Tomato-Caper Sauce

Once veg burger and veg ball are in the sausage lexicon, why not include another offbeat member? In the spirit of having fun stepping outside the box, and for the love of my vegetarian son, Jenan, here is a cabbage leaf–wrapped brown rice, walnut, and dandelion green mix that simulates sausage without the meat. Dandelion greens are the surprise. No matter how young and tender you pick them, they retain a decidedly bitter pucker. But tucked into the brown rice, they cease to affront and instead demur to lending their healthful, herbal kick to the dish. The made-on-the-spur-of-the-moment tomato-caper sauce adds the acid element that brings it all together. **SERVES 6**

1 cup short- or long-grain brown rice, preferably organic

2 ⅓ cups water

1 yellow or white onion, finely chopped

1 cup chopped dandelion greens

½ cup walnuts, toasted and finely chopped

¼ cup chopped fresh flat-leaf parsley

1 tablespoon tomato paste

2 teaspoons kosher salt

½ teaspoon freshly ground black pepper

1 large head cabbage (2 to 3 pounds)

**Sauce**

⅓ cup extra virgin olive oil

1 large tomato, peeled and coarsely chopped, or 2 canned plum tomatoes, coarsely chopped

3 large cloves garlic, coarsely chopped

1 tablespoon capers, preferably salt packed, rinsed

1 tablespoon chopped lemon peel (not just the zest)

Kosher salt

To cook the rice, rinse it, place in a small saucepan, and add 2 cups of the water. Bring to a boil over high heat, cover, and decrease the heat to low. Cook until the water is absorbed and the rice is plumped, 40 to 45 minutes. Set aside off the heat with the lid still on and let steam dry for 10 minutes.

To make the stuffing, bring a small saucepan filled with water to a boil over high heat. Add the onion and dandelion greens and blanch until the onion is translucent, about 2 minutes. Drain and transfer to a large bowl. Add the rice, walnuts, parsley, tomato paste, salt, and pepper, and knead with your hands until thoroughly blended. Set aside at room temperature.

*continued*

To prepare the cabbage leaves, bring a large pot three-fourths full of water to a boil over medium-high heat. Core the cabbage, place it in the pot, cover, and cook until the outer leaves are quite wilted, 15 to 20 minutes. Transfer the cabbage to a colander and set aside until cool enough to handle.

One at a time, gently pull off the cabbage leaves. You should have about 12 leaves of varying sizes. Arrange the leaves, with the inside facing up and the stem end nearest you, on a work surface. Place about 1/4 cup of the stuffing in the center of each leaf. Fold up the bottom of the leaf over the stuffing, then fold in the sides and roll up the leaf to make a tight packet. Arrange the packets, seam sides down, in a single tight layer in a large saucepan. Pour the remaining 1/3 cup water into the pan around, not over, the packets, and place over high heat. Bring to a boil, decrease the heat to maintain a simmer, cover, and cook until the cabbage is very tender, about 25 minutes.

While the packets are cooking, make the sauce. In a large skillet, heat the oil over medium-high heat. Add the tomato, garlic, capers, and lemon peel and stir to mix. Cook until just beginning to boil, then remove from the heat. Season with salt and set aside until ready to use.

To serve, briefly reheat the sauce if desired. Arrange the cabbage packets on a platter and spread the sauce across the top.

# APPENDIX:
## *Grinding Meats and Stuffing Sausage at Home*

## Meats

Not all cuts of meat, whether pork, beef, lamb, or poultry, are suitable for sausage. Here are the cuts to choose for grinding at home.

### Pork

Use shoulder meat, purchased either as a pork butt or pork shoulder roast or as shoulder chops. These cuts are usually trimmed by the butcher and need no further trimming. Pork tenderloin with a little added fat and the fatty ends of pork loin are also good for sausages, but the center-cut loin is not. Use a grinding plate with ⅜-inch holes. This size cuts the meat and its fat just right to make a tender sausage, without smashing either of them or cutting them too large to "melt" when cooked.

### Beef

Look for blade roast, flatiron steak, stew meat, or cross-rib roast. All are cuts of beef chuck and have just the right ratio of meat to fat. Use a grinding plate with ¼- or ⅜-inch holes.

### Lamb

The shoulder, either as shoulder roast, shoulder chops, or sirloin chops, is the most versatile cut for lamb sausage. Occasionally, as in the case of the lamb and bulgur meatballs on page 93, the leaner meat from the leg is desirable. Use a grinding plate with ¼-inch holes.

### Poultry

Purchase either breast meat or thigh meat. An advantage of grinding chicken yourself is that you can include the breast skin, which adds tasty fat. Turkey breast or thigh meat is the choice for sausage making, though I seldom use either cut because turkey is so lean it is not a good candidate for sausage (see page 122 for an exception). Both chicken and turkey usually require added fat of some sort for succulence. Use a grinding plate with ¼- or ⅜-inch holes, depending on how much texture you would like in the sausage.

## Fat

See page 2 for the types of animal fats to use for sausages. For grinding, use the same-size plate as you do for the meat, and put the fat through last, so it can push out any meat left behind in the tube.

## Casings

In shaping sausages, function determines form to a certain extent. That is, in terms of its substance, no difference exists between a patty and a meatball, between a tiny meatball and a large one, or between a link, a patty, and a meatball. But there is an aesthetic difference in the way the dish is perceived, and therefore in the way it is tasted. Following are the options for natural casings and a substitute that is acceptable in a pinch.

### Hog casing and sheep casing

These are the intestines of pigs and sheep, respectively. Hog casing, 1 to 1½ inches in diameter, is used for most sausages, such as sweet Italian, Polish, and so on. Sheep casing, about ½ inch in diameter, is used for small links, such as little breakfast links (page 10) and Creole sausage (page 20). One foot of hog casing holds 8 to 10 ounces of sausage; one foot of sheep casing holds 4 to 6 ounces. They can usually be purchased from butchers who make their own sausage, or both can be ordered on the Internet. They come in salt-encased bundles that will keep almost forever in the refrigerator. Cut off the length you are going to use and rinse thoroughly inside and out by fitting one end on the nozzle of the kitchen sink water spout and gently running water through the casing.

### Caul fat

Also known as veil fat, caul fat is the lining of the lower stomach and upper intestine of pigs or sheep. Pork caul is traditionally used for wrapping *crépinettes* and pâtés, as well as roasts that need some moistening as they cook. Sometimes, you can find a specialty butcher who has it for house use and is happy to sell some to a customer. You can also order it on the Internet in 2- to 5-pound packages. One half pound of caul will wrap about 3½ pounds of sausage in 4-ounce patties. To use caul fat, soak it briefly in lots of water, with distilled white vinegar added if necessary to whiten it, then rinse again. Unravel the caul and spread it out, taking care to handle it gently, as it is quite delicate. Store any caul you haven't used in the freezer indefinitely. If thawed and not used up, caul fat can be refrozen.

### Cheesecloth

For when you want links, not patties or balls, but don't have the casings or equipment for stuffing them, cheesecloth can substitute. It works, with the proviso that it does not lend the unique, desirable flavor that an animal casing does.

To make cheesecloth-wrapped links, divide the sausage mixture into 3- to 4-ounce portions. Press and roll each portion into a log ¾ to 1¼ inches in diameter, depending on the size you want the links. Place each portion in a length of cheesecloth large enough to enclose it, and roll it up snuggly, tucking in the ends as you go. Place the wrapped links on a plate and refrigerate for at least 4 hours; overnight is better. They will keep in the refrigerator for up to 2 days. If you are boiling or parboiling the sausages, leave them in the cheesecloth. Otherwise, unwrap them before sautéing, grilling, or baking.

## Sausage Stuffing

You will need some type of sausage-stuffing device for stuffing sausage mixtures into hog or sheep casing. Various types are available, from simple, hand-cranked countertop models to state-of-the art, highly mechanized apparatuses. When cooks routinely ground their meats and stuffed sausages at home, a hand-cranked meat grinder with a sausage stuffing attachment was part of the kitchen equipment. An electric version of that anachronistic home model makes the job easier and more fun because you don't need to struggle to push the meat through the plate or to fill the casings. For home sausage making, I use an inexpensive electric combination grinder and stuffer. The Internet is full of options in this regard, some with more horsepower, some with less, some taking up a lot of counter space, some more svelte that can be tucked away when not in use. Purchasing one is worth the modest expense if you're avid about stuffing sausages.

For the occasional sausage making impulse, a less expensive way to fill casings is to use a funnel specially designed for sausage stuffing. It has a long nose, so you can thread the casing onto it, and a fairly wide mouth to accommodate a handful of filling at a time. Or, if you want to stuff sausage into casing without employing any special equipment, the ultimate home solution is to use a large-tube regular home funnel or, even more jury-rigged, a plastic bottle with its bottom cut off so you can feed the sausage through. Those are stopgap measures, however; I don't recommend relying on them if you want to stuff sausages more than once or twice. Whichever device you use, thread as much casing onto the funnel end as it will accommodate. Leaving the casing end open—not tied or the sausage will clump, causing air pockets in between—push the sausage through the device into the casing. Smooth out the casing as you go, so the sausage is evenly distributed along its length. Once it is stuffed, smooth out any remaining air pockets and tie a knot at each end. Coil the length or twist it into individual links. If making links, twist each link the opposite way from the one before, to prevent them from coming untwisted.

# INDEX

Greens
  Brown Rice, Walnut, and Dandelion Green Veg Sausage Wrapped in Cabbage Leaves with Tomato-Caper Sauce, 151–52
  Hmong-Style Asian Greens Soup with Beef Meatballs and Slab Bacon, 84–85
Gumbo, Creole Sausage, Shrimp, and Oyster, 21–22

H

Ham Sausage, Chicken Breast Ballotine Stuffed with, 117–18
Harissa, 101
Herbs, 3
Hmong-Style Asian Greens Soup with Beef Meatballs and Slab Bacon, 84–85
Hungarian Meatballs in Paprika Sour Cream with Hungarian Bean Salad, 81–83

I

Italian Sausage, Sweet, 37
  Bread Pizza with Fried Egg and Sausage, 40
  Italian American Spaghetti and Meatballs in Red Sauce, 73
  Pittsburgh-Style Sausage Sandwich with Chunky Tomato and Bell Pepper Sauce, 38

J

Japanese-Style White Fish Balls in Shiitake-Ginger Broth, 142

K

Kebabs, Southeast Asian Pork and Lemongrass Meatball, Wrapped in Lettuce Leaves with Vietnamese Dipping Sauce, 60–61

L

Lamb
  Bell Pepper and Tomato Dolmas with Lamb and Rice Sausage on a Bed of Potatoes, 91
  buying, 1
  Grape Leaves Stuffed with Lamb and Rice Sausage, 92
  Grilled Lamb Sausage in a Pakistani-Style Sandwich with Caramelized Onions, Yogurt, Cilantro, Mint, and Toasted Cumin Seeds, 103–4
  grinding, 153
  Lamb and Bulgur Meatballs in Green Bean and Tomato Soup-Stew, 93–94
  Lamb and Chickpea Meatballs with an Almond Center in Coconut Milk Curry, 95–96
  Lamb and Rice Sausage for Stuffing Leaves and Vegetables, 90
  Merguez, 100
  Merguez and Apple Tagine over Couscous with Harissa, 101–2
  Northern Isles Lamb Sausage, 105
  Scotch Broth with Northern Isles Lamb Sausage, Pearl Barley, and Turnips, 109
  Shepherd's Pie with Northern Isles Lamb Sausage and Potato-Horseradish Crust, 107–8
  Turkish-Style Lamb Sausage with Fig and Fennel Seed Marmalade, 97–99
Leaf lard, 2
Lentils, French, Spicy Garlic Sausage with Chicory and, 51
Lunch Pie, aka Quiche, with Toulouse Sausage and Spinach, 33–34

M

Matzo and Chicken Meatballs in Rich Chicken Broth, 114
Mayonnaise, Dijon, 65–66
Meat. *See also individual meats*
  buying, 1
  grinding, 153
Meatballs
  Beef Polpette with a Cheese Center, 72
  Chicken and Almond Meatballs in White Gazpacho, 115–16
  Chicken and Matzo Meatballs in Rich Chicken Broth, 114
  Hmong-Style Asian Greens Soup with Beef Meatballs and Slab Bacon, 84–85
  Hungarian Meatballs in Paprika Sour Cream with Hungarian Bean Salad, 81–83
  Italian American Spaghetti and Meatballs in Red Sauce, 73
  Lamb and Bulgur Meatballs in Green Bean and Tomato Soup-Stew, 93–94
  Lamb and Chickpea Meatballs with an Almond Center in Coconut Milk Curry, 95–96
  Mexican Meatball Sausage, 27
  Mexican Meatballs in Toasted Garlic–Ancho Chile Broth, 29–30
  Mexican Meatballs Simmered in Tomatillo Sauce with Black Olives, 31
  Porcupine Meatballs with Rice Quills and Hot-Sweet Mustard, 56–58
  Southeast Asian Pork and Lemongrass Meatball Kebabs Wrapped in Lettuce Leaves with Vietnamese Dipping Sauce, 60–61
  Turkey and Pistachio Meatballs in Creamy Chèvre Sauce, 122–23